Wealth is a Mindset

Your Guide to Financial Success

Shikilia Caro

CONTENTS

DEDICATION

I have dedicated this book to the ones I have loved and lost, and from whom I have learned so much. Navigating the conflicting feelings of pain, joy, and grief has helped me to discover my purpose and my passion. I thank each one of you for the love and memories you have given me, and for the lessons learned. You will forever be in my heart and on my mind.

Special Devotion

My grandmother, My Heart

I hope I am making you proud…

ACKNOWLEDGMENT

The process for writing this book required collaboration, support, and understanding from those around me. I am deeply grateful to my family and friends who have pushed me, inspired me, and who took the time to listen as I brainstormed my concepts. The road was longer than I anticipated, but I made it… we made it.

I want to thank those who have taught me lessons along the way. Those who shared their own personal experiences with me. This is for those who get it. My family, my friends, you inspire me in ways that I may never be able to adequately express. I thank God every day for the support and the love I've been so abundantly blessed to receive. Without you all, it would be hard to be totally me. Thank you for being a part of my purpose.

RETIREMENT — **WEALTH** — **LEGACY**

Shiikilia Caro, a native of Northern New Jersey, who relocated to Texas in 1999, is an established financial services professional who provides every client with a legendary service experience. Armed with more than 19 years of experience in her field, Shikilia Caro has proven her ability to manage a diverse portfolio of clients. Her belief that knowledge is the key to a successful financial future has equipped her as a leader, trainer, educator, facilitator, coach, Licensed Real Estate Advisor, and Certified Probate Specialist. She has shared her knowledge and experience with others as a mentor and counselor for the National Association for Black Accountants (NABA), a mentor for Junior Achievement, as well as the VP of Public Relations with Toastmasters. She has also served as Vice Chair on the Ambassador Team for The Arlington Chamber and on the Steering Committee for the Arlington Women's Alliance. Additionally, she's facilitated financial workshops for General Motors, AAA Texas, and Dr. R.W.G Stem Academy, to name a few. She continues her service to the community as a Rotarian, as a member of the Phased-In Foster Care Project, and as Chief Financial Officer on the Board of Directors for RUN Women Cares.

Shikilia began her love and devotion for financial services while studying at Berkley College. Her innate ability to understand each client offers her the opportunity to determine their individual needs, wants & desires. In an effort to diversify her knowledge Shikilia obtained her Texas Real Estate Instructors License to teach Real Estate Finance. Ms. Caro's background, travels, life experience, and commitment to excellent service, has helped her develop the best financial strategies designed to meet each client's current, and more importantly, future needs. Shikilia Caro, continues her journey to establish financially healthy families through one-on-one consultations, workshops and her upcoming book, "Wealth is a Mindset: Your Guide to Financial Success" scheduled for release early 2019.

Workshops

Her speaking topics are designed to develop and support her passion for women's empowerment and entrepreneurial growth while providing a roadmap and keys to success in finance, personal development, and leadership.

Speaking Topics
- Building Your Financial Home "Let's Talk Money"
- 5 Money Mistakes Women Make
- How to Grow Your Money & Spend Your Denaro
- Change Your Mindset & Change Your Money
- Youth & Money Talk

Wealth is a Mindset
- Define your definition of wealth
- Discover your financial mindset
- Develop your road map to financial success

Shikilia Caro

Financial Strategist | Speaker | Realtor | Author
info@sheaassets.com

ABOUT THE AUTHOR

Shikilia Caro, a native of Northern New Jersey, who relocated to Texas in 1999, is an established real estate and financial services professional who provides every client with a legendary service experience. Armed with more than 19 years of experience in her field, Shikilia has proven her ability to manage a diverse portfolio of clients. Her belief that knowledge is the key to a successful financial future has equipped her as a leader, trainer, educator, facilitator, coach, Licensed Real Estate Advisor, and Certified Probate Specialist.

She has shared her knowledge and experience with others as a mentor and a counselor for the National Association for Black Accountants (NABA), a mentor for Junior Achievement, VP of Public Relations with Toastmasters, as well as Chief Financial Officer for RUN Women Cares. She has also served as Vice Chair on the Ambassador Team for The Arlington Chamber of Commerce, and on the Steering Committee for the Arlington Women's Alliance. Additionally, she's facilitated financial workshops for General Motors and Dr. R.W.G Stem Academy, to name a few.

She continues her service to the community as a Rotarian, and as a committee member of the Phased-In Foster Care Project. Shikilia began her love and devotion for financial services while studying at Berkley College. Her innate ability to understand each client offers her the opportunity to determine their individual needs, wants & desires. In an effort to diversify her knowledge, Shikilia obtained her Texas Real Estate Instructors License to teach Real Estate Finance.

Shikilia's background, travels, life experience, and commitment to excellent service, has helped her develop the best real estate and financial strategies designed to meet each client's current, and more importantly, future needs. She continues her journey to establish financially healthy families through one-on-one consultations, workshops, and the book she has authored, *"Wealth Is a Mindset: Your Guide to Financial Success."*

ABOUT THE BOOK

    This book is a compilation of the experiences that Shikilia Caro has navigated throughout her life. Her real estate and financial expertise and compassion for her clients is evident from her works. This book is a unique gem in her long list of accomplishments; a crown jewel in the financial legacy that she wishes to leave behind for future generations.

PREFACE

We often overlook our financial wellbeing in the process of meeting our daily expenses. We rush through our lives without any sort of financial planning. As a result, we suffer several negative consequences, whether we are the ones living through them or our loved ones.

Shikilia Caro's "Wealth Is a Mindset" is out to change the stereotype in people that there is no tomorrow. All you have is today. People need to plan for their future, whether it is their retirement or their death that they are planning for.

Shikilia has shared her years of experience in the financial and real estate industry in her book. She has met many people over the years who made false financial decisions and ended up paying for it with their lives or the livelihood of their loved ones.

She has also helped several people over the years in improving their financial status, and that's exactly what this book will do for you!

Read on to discover how you can meet your personal and financial risks in a timely and effective manner.

CHAPTER 1
SECURITY IS A STATE OF MIND

When we talk about security and being happy, there are a few key elements that cross our minds. These points revolve around a person's physical, mental, and financial health. These points also relate to the quality of one's life and how that person views success, as well as how they define security.

Improvement in Quality of Life – A Step towards Creating Security

A person's quality of life is also associated with the temperament of the people involved in their lives. In addition, one must care about themselves if they seek to live a pleasant life. This sense of fulfilment not only adds happiness, but enhances the perspective that person has about themselves, putting them in a better social standing. Since sound mental health is a major part of what it takes to be and stay happy, it is vital for every individual to pay close attention to their own moods and behaviors.

The brain, like any other organ in the body, should get regularly scheduled wellness checkups. Our mental health is often referred to as our overall psychological well-being. Mental health encapsulates the way we feel about ourselves, our finances, and other people in our surroundings. Our mental condition affects our ability to manage our feelings and behaviors. It influences how we deal with difficulties, trials and tribulations.

Being mentally and emotionally healthy is a lot more than not having depression, anxiety, or any other psychological issue. In fact, when there is no such mental illness present, we have an opportunity to make room to add positive characteristics to our mindset.

A famous author, Stephen Covey, highlighted in his book that security represents your sense of worth, your identity, your emotional anchorage, your self-esteem, your basic personal strength or the lack of it. For some people, success is achieving a $60,000 per year income. For someone else it may be saving $1,000,000 by a certain age. For another person, it may be raising successful children or securing a particular position on the corporate ladder.

What is success to you? How do you define it? Take a moment to think about what gives you a sense of security.

However, before you think really hard about this, know one thing. Your mental health or your state of mind determines your sense of security, regardless of how things are in your life at the moment.

How does Your State of Mind affect Your Sense of Security?

The moment your state of mind determines your sense of security, your subconscious takes you in the direction you need to go to build the same security in practical life.

Here, your thought process becomes of utmost importance.

Following are a few ways in which you can build a healthy state of mind. Think of these things when you feel your state of mind wavering:

- Irrespective of how happy you are on your own, improvement in your emotional health will be boosted only through social interaction with other people. This is because we are social creatures who have emotional needs for relationships and a desire to have positive connections with others. It is not in our nature to thrive in isolation. Our brains crave companionship. Even if we are shy and/or our past experiences are not favorable, people will still desire to converse and interact with other people. You have to build interactions that are positive and that keep you positive and motivated. Ask yourself; are you satisfied with your relationships?
- The mind and the body are intrinsically linked. When you

work on your physical health, it automatically places you on the path for greater mental and emotional health. Physical activity also releases endorphins, otherwise known as feel-good chemicals. These powerful chemicals have the ability to lift your mood and provide you with greater energy to get through your day actively. Regular exercise or physical activity can positively impact the mental and emotional health of any person. Physical exertions help in relieving stress, improving memory, and even giving you a good night's sleep. Ask yourself; are you in-tune with your physical health? Are you conscience about what you put in your body and how often you engage in physical activities?

- Stress has the capacity to give a heavy blow to an individual's mental and emotional health. Hence it is important for you to keep your stress levels in control. Let's face facts; it is not realistic that all types of stress be avoided. But stress management strategies can help you bring things back into balance. Ask yourself; what element of your life is currently bringing you stress; is it your finances, relationships, health concerns; how are you going to move forward to reduce said stress? Keep in mind that the way we view our situations have great impact on the stress level relative to the situation.

- Unless you have had drastic changes in your diet in the past, you may not be aware of just how much the food you take or avoid can have on your mental health and the way you feel. An unhealthy diet can make your brain function slower, disrupt your sleeping pattern, take away your energy, and also dwindle your immune system. Similarly, adopting a wholesome diet which is low in sugar and rich in healthy fats, can provide you with plenty of benefits. This dieting choice provides you with more energy, your sleeping behavior improves, and it helps you in looking and feeling your best. The best place for starting on your dieting journey is beginning to eat healthy foods and by cutting out the "*bad fats*". These fats can damage your mood and your overall health. You would need to replace them with "*good fats*" that support brain-health and your overall performance.

- People with busy schedules often compromise on their sleep in an effort to focus on work. When done regularly it can have terrible aftereffects on both your physical and mental health. Skipping even a few hours of sleep will affect your mental sharpness, mood, energy, and the ability to counter stress. If the lack of sleep persists, then long-term consequences are even more sinister. Chronic sleep loss can wreak havoc on your health with irregularities occurring in your digestion, immune system, blood pressure and can even lower your sex drive. So, let your brain rest in-order to maintain a happy heathy life. Ask yourself; do you feel rested or sluggish when you rise to start your day?

- Having meaning and having purpose in various ways is liberating. Especially when we are doing things that benefit others, as well as ourselves. Whether it makes us feel needed or just good about ourselves, whichever way we look at it, having a purpose drives us forward. Having a purpose can be a reason to get out of bed in the morning. Not only is having purpose a spiritually satisfying thing, but it also has biological benefits. Finding meaning and purpose is vital to our brain's health as it can increase the generation process of new cells and neural pathways in the brain. It also strengthens our immune system, while alleviating pain and relieving stress levels in the body. As a result, it can have an enormous effect on our financial health as well. No matter what way you look at purpose, it helps to give meaning to life. Ask yourself; have you found your purpose? What legacy do wish to leave behind? How do you want your name to be relevant to your great-great-great grandchildren? Does the reputation you have in your community shine a positive light on your character? Are you more of a giver than a taker? How do you contribute to the betterment of not just yourself, but of those around you?

In order for your mind to have perceived security, these aforementioned aspects must be present so that you can live a peaceful life that leads you to success. The better equipped you are with the above traits, you will have a happier, more peaceful life. You will be able to experience stability, sustainability and soundness in your life like never before. The closer you will move in the direction of security and prosperity. You will have an improved quality of life.

Many people confuse quality of life with standard of living. True, the enhancement of financial wellbeing contributes immensely to improving our way of living. However, it is not the only parameter for improving our quality of life. In fact, you can say that an improved quality of life can help in maintaining excellent financial stability. We must strive to check as many boxes for prosperity and success as is possible. These characteristics are qualities which will assist us with developing a positive outlook on life. In fact, you will enjoy sharing this positivity with other people.

How do You Acquire A Sense of Security in Your Life?

Now that we have identified the road towards our way for achieving a healthy mind, we can work on acquiring a sense of security. A sense of security may differ from person to person. One thing that remains constant is that lack of having security can have dire consequences on your mental and physical wellbeing.

When you are certain and secure about your direction and your finances, it will bring a sense of calmness into your life and protection. A sense calmness will enable you to divert your attention into more positive things. The sense of security can be reflective in several areas of your life. You could be looking for emotional security, security surrounding your social life, financial security or even security surrounding your religious life. It all depends on your needs at the time.

Emotional Security Leading to Financial Security

There are multiple ways for you to achieve emotional security. One easily distinguishable trait for establishing emotional security is *having* love for others and *being* loved by others. Sometimes, the fear of being alone is tied with assumptions and beliefs about experiencing a lack of love for ourselves and for others. Such beliefs usually arise due to feelings of being unworthy, rejection of ourselves and the rejection of other people who may or may not deserve it. In order to escape from this painful emotion, most people seek protection and safety in other ways.

Although there have been many times when we have been alone and been happy, most of us tend to do better in the company of others. This way we will have more people to appreciate us when we do something good. In the same way we will be surrounded by, mentors, coaches, consultants, advisors, and spiritual counselors when we don't do as well. No one can survive without companionship. The best athletes always have a coach. The best speakers have mentors for life. Even the president has his Chief of Staff.

All of *"The Greats"* have a coach, in some form or fashion, to seek guidance and advisement from, especially when they are moving in the wrong direction. Of course, ultimately, you are responsible for creating your own happiness and success. Often there is some input from a team, a support system, a partner. There are multiple contributing factors to that type of emotional connection and trust. These characteristics include being self-aware.

You must be aware of the strength of your individual characteristics and the vulnerabilities you possess. In addition to that, you must also know what you need to feel safe and secure. You must have enough confidence to trust yourself and not be paralyzed by fear. You must trust yourself to look out for your own best interests without being dependent on someone else.

You must know that you are also capable of creating your own emotional, physical, energetic, spiritual, and financial boundaries. When you begin making decisions and taking steps to move your life forward, you become more secure and more aware of how things may pan out and how to deal with problems should they arise. When developing your individual road map, remember that there is nothing wrong with having a professional *"coach"* to assist you with the decision-making process.

Defining Success

Here is my personal definition of success...There are many ways of achieving success and every person has their own story. Yet, for some people, it is hard for them to tell their own story because they are either waiting for the right signs to appear so that they can start their success story, or they are looking at success through someone else's lens. Some hesitate to take forward moving steps in fear of risking too much.

But history shows us that you cannot get anywhere while you are being controlled by fear. Definitions of success and security vary from person to person, which makes it a debatable subject. For me, security is defined as a healthy work-personal-spiritual life balance and the accomplishment of my goal to increase my annual income by a minimum of 10% per annum. I also find security in knowing that I can achieve whatever I set out to achieve, as long as what I am trying to achieve aligns with my purpose. My purpose is the plan that God has preordained for my life. No one can achieve success without taking risks and learning through trial and error.

Proverbs 24:16 states *"For though the righteous fall seven times, they rise again, but the wicked stumble when calamity strikes."*

We must learn to view failure simply as lessons of what not to do. We cannot allow fear to paralyze our progression. Here are a few principles to follow that may help you achieve your desired success. They have helped me consistently in my life. Maybe they can do the same for you!

Setting Goals

People who have a certain idea of what they want and have set a course for achieving their goals are generally happier in comparison to those who have no plan for their future. This is not a very unique concept. In fact, it's often the basis of any material intended to direct and motivate. In context of this, Powell expressed that, *"There are no secrets to success. It is the result of preparation, hard work, and learning from failure."*

I generally have specific goals in my mind that can tackle anything that I know I will be facing in the near future, while aligning my path with my long-term goals. I try hard to be ready for *"the pivot"* when life throws me a curve. I maintain a Plan B & C, while preparing myself for the worst-case-scenario. I know there is a lot of debate surrounding whether or not a person should have a Plan B. But, for me, having a pre-planned direction to pivot in has worked to my benefit. Take for example the crash of the real estate market in 2008. I was a self-employed Realtor and Loan Officer back then. When the market crashed, and I was forced to shut down my business, I was able to reach into my back pocket to retrieve my insurance hat.

I had been an insurance underwriter for almost seven years prior to going into real estate. I was able to take that skill set, my Plan B, and enter back into Corporate America. I still managed to operate a portion of my real estate business on the side while employed, but the ability to pivot provided me with a safe-haven while I rebounded. After some time, I was able to regain my position back on Track/Plan A.

Note, just because you take a detour, it does not mean that you can't resume your position when the time aligns with your purpose. People often call this pivot an inconsistency. I call it moving forward and doing what you have to do in the meantime. Often your pivot is just a delay, not a setback. Most often, our delays are blessings wrapped in a trial, disguised as a tribulation. In some cases, it just wasn't the right time

Fearing Failure

Often, the fear of failing stops people from trying different things. Adding to the equation is the fear of being made fun of. However, we must realize that there is no sure shot one way of doing anything right. The cycle of success goes along with failure and trying, resulting on in greater success. We only make progress by taking risks and learning from previous mistakes.

Not fearing failure for me is knowing that as long as I am healthy and breathing, I have an opportunity to try again, perhaps using a different approach. If you keep that in mind, then you will undoubtedly make it easier to achieve your goals. Nobody expects you to charge mindlessly into unexplained territory. It is good to prepare yourself for situations that you may face. Preparation will reduce the amount of fear and anxiety you may have when approaching an intimidating situation. But not everything can be anticipated when trying something new. So, expect the unexpected and know that whatever you may face, you must keep moving forward!

Learning Process

When planning to succeed, the learning process must NOT stop. The more you learn, the greater will be your hunger to explore new insights. An inaccurate belief is that once you have reached your definition of success, you have learned everything you need to know, which is not true. Hence, you must always continue to learn about new developments in your area(s) of interest.

Having a mission to continuously learn will help you in achieving your goals effectively. Knowledge, no matter how insignificant it may appear, can give you great understanding for your future endeavors. Having the ability to see things from multiple perspectives can help you with critical thinking and problem-solving skills. You should try to learn something new each and every day so that you can remain on the path of continuous progress and enlightenment.

Treat knowledge as your new friend and not as a nuisance. There is a quote by Bill Gates; *"Success is a lousy teacher. It seduces smart people into thinking they can't lose."* It truly encapsulates how success teaches us things but not always in the best possible ways. It teaches us that those who think that they know everything truly will only be faced with the harsh reality that they, in fact, are living in delusion. It is said that you must ask questions in order to gain understanding. Be an expert in your field by having an open mind and staying in *"the know"* about your respective industry. Stay abreast of current affairs, rules, and regulations. Always be open to learning new things, even if the lesson is coming from a child. Taking notes is a key component to learning new things. You never know when you may have to revisit that point of reference. In addition to the above-mentioned rules for success, there were a few things that I learned during my journey.

The basic rule is to surround yourself with people who encourage you to learn more, who adds value to your life, and who have some understanding about what it is that you are doing and looking to accomplish. If you are not surrounded by encouraging people, you may find it a little more challenging to achieve your goals. Negative people will surely disrupt and hinder your journey. Another thing that I learned is that it makes life much easier when we have our financial goals in place and we are working on them with an actual *"track to run on"* or a direction to go in.

The more focused we are on our financial prosperity, the harder we will strive to achieve our goals. When you already have an idea or a set of goals for what you want to earn, save, invest and spend, you will find that the steps you take for achieving them fall right in line with your overall picture of success. You must set monthly, weekly, or even yearly goals so that you can work daily to achieve them. You know you may be capable of achieving great things, but you will never truly do any of that until you actually try. Then you will see what you are really made of.

My Story

My personal meaning of success has been adjusted over the years based on my experiences and my level of maturity. At the age of 16, I was promoted to manager at a local record store while attending high school. After high school, I was hired as a bank teller while I attended school at night. At the age of 20, I was hired at a reputable insurance company as an assistant, soon promoted to customer service representative and ultimately promoted to underwriter, now traveling to train others. By the time I was 30 years old, I had relocated to another state and had begun my career as an entrepreneur.

Soon after that I was married with a large extended family. I want to lay it out for you to demonstrate how changing priorities have a ripple effect on our goals, resulting in adjustments to our definition of success and security. You must sit down periodically throughout the year to evaluate what you have achieved thus far, and what's next on your list.

You cannot undo the past, but you can make proper adjustments today to plan for a better tomorrow. If you are not where you would like to be financially, what's that plan? If you have not planned properly for your children's education, what's the plan? If you have not taken steps to properly protect your income, what's the plan?

If you have not planned for your parent's and your own long-term care, what's the plan? If you have not given legal instructions for taking care of your children should you not make it back home one day, it's not too late. You must start from where you are today... Step-by-step, you can reach your personal definition of success!

CHAPTER 2
LIFE INSURANCE IS FOR LIVING

Many people do not take the initiative to purchase insurance unless they are forced to purchase it. Let's take auto insurance as an example. Although auto insurance protects your vehicle, the other vehicle(s), personal property, and the lives and injuries of people and animals involved in a motor vehicle accident, a great number of people still would not take auto insurance protection if it were not required by law.

Most often people only purchase insurance when a rule or law requires them to do so, or when they, or someone they know, have experienced a loss. In the case of life insurance, if you wait until you feel you *"need"* life insurance, it may very well be too late. Given the fact that the cost of life insurance is determined by one's age and health, waiting until you feel you *"need"* it would probably mean you are much older and/or have developed some type of illness. In some cases, a person's age or health could render them uninsurable.

That means that you can develop a condition for which insurance companies deem too high of a risk to cover. With that said, the cost of life insurance and your ability to be covered, will never be cheaper than it is today. In the case of a loss on large ticketed items, such as your home, vehicle, appliances, jewelry, and most of all the lives of those you would be responsible for should something happen to them, should hasten you to carry the proper type of insurance, and the proper amount of insurance.

Carrying proper insurance would negate you from shelling out money from your savings and long-term investment vehicles when losses occur. Having insurance policies for the things you value the most, should most definitely include your life and the lives of your loved ones.

There are a variety of plans which cover almost anything that is of value to you, and all of them have varied payment and pay out options.

The Right Time to Purchase Life Insurance

How does one determine the right time to purchase life insurance? Well let me ask this one very simple question. Can you determine when you may have an accident? Can you determine when you may be diagnosed with a critical illness? Can you determine when your end of days will occur? Since the timing of not one of those things can be predetermined, then we must ascertain that the right time to protect ourselves is NOW.

As mentioned earlier, there are multiple benefits to buying a life insurance policy at a younger age rather than at an older age. Not purchasing a life insurance policy at a young age can be costly over the long run. The cost of a ten-year term policy purchased for someone at the age of 30 using an amount of $100,000, could be as little as $288 per year. This amount may differ with regards to the gender of the person and their health conditions. On the other hand, the annual premium for a 40-year-old male could cost $468 per year. The accumulated cost of delaying purchase by 10 years over the life of the policy is about $1,800.

As mentioned earlier, the cost of purchasing life insurance is greater if the person is older. There is also a greater likelihood that medical conditions have developed as an individual ages. If you already have a serious medical condition, a policy can be rated high risk by the life insurance underwriter. This could lead to even higher premium payments and there is also a possibility that the application for coverage can be declined outright. In order to get maximum benefit at the best price, getting coverage before the age of 30 is your best bet. Before the age of 30, is prime time to invest in such a program.

Unfortunately, many people at that age are usually more worried about their student loan debts and rent. Therefore, they put off placing proper protections in place. They don't realize how much this positioning is going to cost them over time. Many young people question their need to purchase life insurance. They figure that at this point in their lives they don't need it; they have time. They can just wait until they are older and *"closer to being a senior citizen"* which means closer to death in so many words.

Some of them don't yet have a family to care for and therefore are confused as to who should benefit from their life insurance policy. What they may not realize is that the process for changing the names of beneficiaries is fairly easy and can be changed as often as necessary as you cycle through life and your needs change. In the event that you do not have your own family, you can name the person closest to you who you would trust to handle your affairs. This could be your siblings, your parents, your significant other, a charitable organization, or a friend as your beneficiary.

This early step has another benefit apart from just keeping the premiums low. It will also enable you to buy a lot more insurance coverage than you may be able to acquire in later years of your life. In addition to that, there could be a possibility that you could develop health conditions at an early age. This means that your family may already be at a risk of losing you and any security they have from your presence. Purchasing coverage early on, protects your ability to be insured.

Who Benefits?

Primarily the one who benefits from the life insurance policy is the one whose name is written as the beneficiary by the person who purchased the policy. Beneficiaries receive the exact amount designated by the policy owner. With this coverage in place, there is assurance that the financial needs of your loved ones will be taken care of and that they can continue to live comfortably whether you are with them or you have passed on.

I call this loving from beyond! Providing for your family should not stop at the grave. Your loved ones would be facing a lot of hardships if God forbid, you suddenly pass away. They would be dealing with grief that no amount of money could ease. But, the least you can do for them, even after you're gone, is to make sure that they have enough money to bury you and take care of your final expenses while grieving at the same time.

There are many final expenses, aside from burial, that most people don't consider. For instance, where would you want to be buried? If it is in another state or far off town, there is a cost to transport you there. There is a cost to release a body from the morgue. The tombstone is very costly. There is a cost associated with packing and moving your things. There are balances you may share with someone that is now going to be left solely on that person. Someone may have cosigned a student loan, mortgage, or auto loan for you; that person is still going to have to pay. There are many ways that the beneficiaries can use the amount that is paid to them. Hopefully, the amount paid out is more than enough to cover just the funeral.

Purchasing the right policy to cover your particular circumstances are crucial. The policy should cover all types of possible causes of death... be it accidental, natural, or an act of murder. If you do have young children who plan to go to college, then taking care of their college tuition should be an intricate part of your planning.

How endearing would it be to place your children in a position not to have to worry about student loans that you are not here to cosign for? This would avoid the financial burden that is often placed on young people before they even start their careers. Life insurance enjoys favorable tax treatment unlike financial instruments. Which is why it's a great place to start for anyone looking to leave a financial legacy behind. Furthermore, the benefits may include several tax advantages.

Living Benefits

As the name implies, living benefits are advantages derived from a life insurance policy that the owner benefits from while they are still alive. There are many policies that allow the owner to reap benefits from the policy they've purchased. This does not mean that your beneficiaries won't be benefitting from your life insurance, but you can benefit before the beneficiaries get to benefit. Here are some of the living benefits that can be realized with the purchase of a life insurance policy:

Accelerated Death

An Accelerated Death Benefit (ADB) or Terminal Illness Rider is a benefit attached to a life insurance policy that enables the policy holder to receive a cash advance against the death benefit in the case of being diagnosed with a terminal illness. If the insured is diagnosed with a terminal illness and told that he/she has less than twelve months to live, the owner can access up to 50% of the face amount (in most cases) while still living. The named beneficiaries would be paid the balance.

Now you're terminally ill... This advance could help you pay medical bills, pay for experimental medications and treatments that insurance won't cover, household bills that are piling up due to your illness, or to just knock some things off your bucket list. On the other hand, it can also be used for you to live the time you have left comfortably at your home. The choice is yours in that matter!

Cash Accumulation

There are policies with cash accumulation accounts. These are policies wherein a portion of the policy premiums are going into an account which can grow at a particular interest rate. This cash can be taken out of the policy by way of loans or withdrawals as it accumulates during the life of the policy.

These funds can be used to pay college tuitions, for various business ventures, weddings, the purchase of a home, retirement, or anything else the owner deems important. These funds can be used while still providing a death benefit for your loved ones, making sure they remain safe from being at a disadvantage when you're no longer here.

There are also policies that offer a return of premium. These are policies for which you pay a higher premium to ensure that all of the funds you have paid in over the years are refunded back to you at the end of the policy term.

Tax Shelter

Having a life insurance policy gives you protections that no investment can give you. It provides the ability to transfer a policy's death benefit free of any income tax to the named beneficiaries. In most cases, whether the amount payable is $50,000 or a whopping $5 million, your beneficiaries usually will not have to pay income taxes on the funds they are awarded.

The tax-deferred growth of the cash accumulating in the cash account of your life insurance policy is not vulnerable to the Social

Security Administration or Medicare. You can use your funds to supplement your retirement income, pay for any medical care you may need, etc. Life insurance policies are one of the few items that are exempted from taxation on your Social Security income. And as mentioned earlier, if your policy permits, you are able to take tax-free loans from your cash account.

Life Insurance Vs. Cash and Other Assets

There are certain possessions that you own in life which have the potential to pay you back or provide you with financial security. Assets are something that you purchase, and you expect those things to still have value in the future. Possessing an asset does not necessarily mean it will grow in value. In fact, some assets such as a car or an electronic device will diminish in value over time. In an ideal situation, the value of the asset you own will increase over time. Usually assets such as a house or shares of a stock increase in value, therefore increasing the chances of getting a good pay out from them when and if you do sell them.

Cash is something that is used as an exchange for goods and services. Its value is dependent on the economics of the country, its GDP (Gross Domestic Product) and the amount of debt it is in. Fluctuating economies can result in the growth or deflation of the value of any currency. This enables a chain reaction throughout the country where the prices of the things being imported, exported and being sold to consumers throughout the country are adjusted. Situations like this happen over time and do not usually happen overnight unless the country has faced a major setback.

In both scenarios, there are chances of our assets losing value and our finances and investments dwindling. As a solution, add a fixed insurance product to the equation. With a fixed insurance product, there is a minimum interest rate to be paid no matter what the market does. This approach secures your principal against any losses that the rising or falling economy of your country may bring with it. Although the dividends paid, or the cash in the account may accumulate at a slower rate, you are guaranteed to see some type of growth. This is where we keep our *"safe money"*. Safe money represents the money that we don't choose to gamble with. This is money that we would like to protect against any type of loss.

The Nursing Home Nightmare

Caleb Lawrence was a man with incredible wealth. He was the owner of a few of the best hotels in the country. They all housed luxurious lobbies, fine dining restaurants and had high class suites. His hotels were ones where not only Hollywood stars would come to stay, but they were also frequented by powerful politicians, sports personalities, and many rich billionaire business tycoons. He was living a comfortable life in his mansion that was worth over $5 million in San Francisco, California. Caleb lived there with his lovely wife, Natalie, his 10-year old son Jeremy, and an army of servants. Things were perfect for this family, as they did not have a care in the world. They had enough money to spend hundreds of thousands of dollars on a fleet of personal vehicles, while still comfortably living an extravagant lifestyle of travel and entertainment. This sense of false security led Caleb to believe that he could counter any threat that may come his way by using his large bank accounts; after all, he had successfully overcome all challenges to this point.

Caleb did not believe in life insurance because he was financially secure with plenty of excess. He believed that he was earning enough to adequately provide for his family in any circumstance. But fate had other plans for him. His decision-making process was slowly beginning to falter and he started to notice it for himself. He was starting to become very forgetful. He couldn't remember where he had placed things, what he had eaten for breakfast, and conversations with his family, friends, and colleagues.

They all started noticing that something was truly wrong. Caleb finally decided that he needed to consult his doctor with the matter. It was then that he was diagnosed with the Alzheimer's disease. The doctor told him up front that the disease was in the initial stage and that it would spread with time. He would also have to face the fact that his condition will never improve, but in fact will only get worse over time.

This was a total shock for him as he had never considered the possibility of an illness that could end life as he knew it. He had always thought that death would be quick and painless. But in this situation, the doctor informed him that he would slowly decline over a 6 to 20-year period. He quickly realized that he would have to watch himself get closer and closer to death every day.

He informed his family about his situation. They stuck in there and kept him at home for as long as possible. They kept him home until his condition started to require around the clock care. His wife soon had to place him in a nursing home where he could be cared for more efficiently. Slowly, over the course of a year, his condition got worse and now he was at a point where he could not even sign his own name.

Soon, just like his health, his business started deteriorating and the person he had chosen to run the business did not live up to expectations. About eight years after Caleb learned about his disease, his wife was forced to sell the business to stay afloat. Approximately four years after that, his stay at home wife had to sell the family home. Since all of Caleb's fortune was taxable and deemed as earned income, the nursing home where Caleb was housed was able to drain his accounts to pay for his care. Fifteen years after Caleb entered the nursing home he passed away. He had not considered the cost associated with long-term care.

There is no way he could have anticipated needing that kind of care for fifteen whole years. By the time Caleb passed on, he left his wife homeless and penniless. She had to move in with her son, where she remains to this day. Had Caleb purchased a life insurance policy, or any other type of policy protected under the life insurance umbrella, those funds would have been protected and would not have counted in his asset calculation. He would have qualified sooner for government assistance with his care, prior to all of his funds being totally depleted.

His wife could have used the money accumulating in the cash account without the funds being considered earned income by the nursing home. In addition, the death proceeds would have passed on to her, giving her the shelter and security she needed to remain independent.

CHAPTER 3
TYPES OF LIFE INSURANCE

There are multiple ways to insure your belongings and yourself. Each type of insurance has their own unique benefits, terms, and conditions. Since life insurance is one of the most important and the one with the longest coverage terms in the industry, it offers multiple options. The type of life insurance that is best for each person should be determined by that individual's lifestyle, anticipated final expenses, mortgage balance, the number of years left to pay on said mortgage, other debts such as car note balances, credit cards, student loan balances, the need to provide a college fund for young children, and any special considerations that an individual may have.

A special consideration could be providing additional funds to take care of a special-needs child, providing for a parent's elder care, the need to make special arrangements for pets, providing a succession plan for a business, or leaving donations to a particular charitable organization or to a church. The type of life insurance offered is also determined by whether or not the individual currently has some life insurance in place, and whether or not the family will also be benefiting from other vehicles such as a CD, stocks, bonds, or a 401K plan. Age, health, budget and affordability are also major factors in determining the right product for a particular person. In essence, recommendations for each plan should be tailored specifically towards meeting the needs of that individual. Selecting the right type and amount of coverage should never be random. A customized plan is the right way to go.

Keep in mind that as life continues to cycle, the needs of an individual may change. That is why it is very important that needs of the policy owner are assessed on an annual basis. It is in our best interest to keep our coverage updated and tailored toward our most current needs. It is amazing what could happen in a one-year period.

A child could be born, another child could graduate from college, the mortgage could be paid off, one could get married or divorced, a home could be purchased or sold, one could start a business or sell a business, and a host of other things could occur, just to name a few. When circumstances change, there may be a need to change named beneficiaries, reduce or increase the amount of insurance in force, or add a different type of coverage to the portfolio.

Let's take a look at the types of plans offered in the market.

Term Life Insurance

As Ramanathan (2015) explains, term insurance is the simplest and the oldest form of insurance. It requires payment of the face amount or death benefit to the beneficiary of the deceased, in the case that the death of the insured occurs within the policy term period. If the person insured lives beyond the term period that is stated in the insurance policy, then the purchaser will be at a loss. This is because term insurance has an expiration date. Therefore, the insurance company is not liable to pay outside of the stated policy term.

Because term insurance is simply *"just in case"* protection, the premium amounts that were paid will not be refunded. Term insurance is put in place *"just in case"* you pass away during the covered period. This type of insurance is great for providing protection for temporary situations, such as to cover a mortgage obligation. If you have a 30-year mortgage for $250K, you would want to make sure that the term policy remains in force for 30 years so that if something happens to you within that 30-year period, the home would be paid off for your family. This is a temporary situation being covered by a temporary policy that will expire once the debt has been paid. That way, you are not paying for coverage you no longer need. This specific type of insurance is very similar to the premiums you pay for your car insurance. In the way that if there is no claimable event, there is no benefit to be paid. Another similar benefit to auto insurance is the peace of mind that term insurance provides during the protection period. Term life insurance is pure insurance and nothing more. Almost 100% of the premiums that are paid to the provider are used to cover the cost of the insurance.

Because people are living longer, a large percentage of people are outliving their term policies. In the US, around 80% of the term policies are never paid out. That means that term policies are often very profitable for insurance companies. This affords the insurance companies the ability to offer the product at a much lower price point. Premiums on term insurance are much lower than any other life insurance product for this reason. That is why you are able to purchase a policy with a large face amount at a very reasonable cost. In addition to the basic coverage described, term policies have their own set of variants to choose from.

Renewable Term Assurance – This clause is also known as a Renewable Term and an Annual Renewable Term. It is a one-year contract that allows the owner of the policy to extend the coverage term for a set period of time without having to requalify for coverage. This offers a guarantee of future insurability for a set number of years. It is contingent on premium payments being up to date. As the insured person ages, premiums increase. This is most often the least expensive way to get coverage started. However, it is very costly over the long run.

Level Premium Term Insurance - It is a policy where premiums payable throughout the term of the policy remain the same, while the face amount, or amount payable is leveled as well. This will eliminate payment of premiums that increase year after year. It is most commonly available for periods ranging from 10 years to 30 years.

Convertible Term Insurance – This is a clause that can be used by persons being insured initially by a pure term insurance policy that offers an option to later convert into a different type of plan without going through the underwriting approval process all over again. For example, the policyholder can convert a term insurance policy into a permanent whole life policy in accordance with the conditions stated in the original policy. There are reasons why a person may take this route. It could be that the person wishes to purchase permanent insurance, but affordability may be an issue at the time. In an effort to protect the insured person's ability to qualify for coverage, they could purchase a policy more fitting to the current budget. When circumstances change, and affordability is no longer an issue, the policy owner could then exercise the right to convert to a plan that does not have an expiration date. Keep in mind that the premium will change in accordance with the newly selected plan.

Term Insurance with Return of Premiums - This term insurance rider combines coverage and the element of a savings together. The premiums paid into the policy are returned to the owner if the person insured survives the policy term and no claims are made. Premiums for this policy are higher than other term products because some portion of the premiums paid are invested in order for the company to be able to return the amount paid into the policy back to the policy owner at the end of the policy term.

Term Insurance with Guaranteed Renewal – This clause states that at the end of the initial term, the policy owner has the option to renew the policy, regardless of the changes to the health of the person insured. No further proof of insurability such as a medical examination is required. Premiums often increase significantly when exercising this benefit. They sometimes double and triple over the original premium outlay.

Decreasing Term Insurance - With this type of term insurance, the face amount, or amount of coverage, steadily decreases with each passing year. This normally matches the decreasing need for the insurance covering a specific need. This type of policy is normally selected when the purchaser of the policy has taken out a large loan, to either buy a house or a similar investment. Since there is a risk of the person passing away before fully repaying the loan, this type of policy can be put in place to pay the outstanding loan balance. Hence, the sum payable in the policy is usually an amount that is equal to the amount of the loan balance to be paid. The policy term is also equal to the time-period in which the loan is to be repaid. As you pay the loan back, the sum to be paid under the policy also decreases to match the outstanding loan balance. An example of a decreasing term policy would be a pure, traditional Mortgage Insurance Policy. As the mortgage balance decreases, the benefit amount to be paid also decreases. In most cases, benefits are paid directly to the mortgage company as beneficiary, not to your loved one.

Whole Life (WL) Insurance - A whole life policy is a permanent product intended to provide coverage for a lifetime. Whole life policies offer cash values that can earn interest and pay dividends. One of the best advantages of having this type of policy is that it can never decrease in value unless the cash values are withdrawn from the policy. The value may also decrease or be terminated if you stop paying your premiums. In short, a whole life policy can be used as a vehicle to accumulate cash while benefiting from the tax shelters that life insurance affords. When premiums are paid, a portion of those funds go toward the cost of insurance. The remaining premium amount goes towards increasing the cash value. The premiums paid on whole life policies are paid with after-tax dollars. The cash value grows without taxation. However, you may be subjected to taxation on policy withdrawals that exceed the amount you have paid into the policy. As an additional benefit, the policy offers loan options. Taking funds from the policy in the form of a loan avoids taxation in most instances. Most whole life policies pay a dividend. These dividends aren't taxed but are considered returns of premium. So, for example if your insurance company pays out $1,000 in dividends on your policy at the end of the year, you are not required to pay taxes on that money. You can re-invest those funds into the cash value of the policy, or you can use the funds to purchase additional paid-up life insurance. This means that you will be able to increase the policy's living benefit as well as its death benefit by increasing the policy's cash value. Paid-up additions can earn dividends as well, meaning that their value compounds over time. In order to decide whether whole life insurance works for you or not, you must have a clear perspective as to why you are buying insurance. Whole Life is a great option in the case where you have a need for long-term insurance, and also would like to supplement your retirement. Before selecting this policy, it is best to map out exactly what your overall finances are. Furthermore, it is always best to consult a financial professional who is aware of all of your needs, and concerns before making this decision.

Universal Life (UL) Insurance - Universal life is similar in some ways to whole life insurance. The potential advantage of the universal life policy is its flexibility and the potential for greater cash value growth if the interest rates offered outperform the insurer's general account. Universal life is more flexible than whole life in two primary ways; the death benefit, and the fact that usually the premium payments are flexible. The death benefit can be increased (subject to insurability) and decreased without surrendering the policy or getting a new one as would be required with whole life. Also, a range of premium payments can be made to the policy, from a minimum amount to cover various guarantees that the policy may offer, to the maximum amount allowed by IRS rules. The primary difference is that the universal life policy shifts some of the risk for maintaining the death benefit to the insured. Secondly, there are more flexible exit strategies within a Universal Life contract which increases the flexibility of that contract over the Whole Life policy. Universal Life is used as a tax-advantaged way to purchase life insurance. In the early years of the contract, the premium far exceeds the cost of insurance (COI) charges. The difference between the two (the *"inside build-up"*) will grow tax-deferred so long as the policy remains in force. If the policy is held until death, this inside build-up will escape taxation entirely. This is because you paid the premium with after-tax money, so the money going in has already been taxed. Therefore, only growth would be taxed. However, since you only pay taxes on the growth, and you rarely see growth relative to premiums paid, most often, the money in the end is able to escape taxation. Policyholders may also be able to access the inside build-up via a policy loan without incurring it as taxable income for the same reason.

Notes

Whole life insurance – Caters to long-term goals by offering consumers consistent premiums and guaranteed cash value accumulation.

Universal life insurance – Gives consumers flexibility in the premium payments, death benefits, and the cash accumulation element of their policies.

Life Diamond Story

At the age of 45, Gary was living a wonderful life. He had a prosperous career, a lovely wife, Jessica, and three lovely daughters, Ariana, Sophie, and Kate. Ariana was the eldest at age 16, while Sophie was the middle child at age 14, and Kate was 12 years old and the youngest of the three. With the girls at such tender ages, the family encountered a stroke of bad luck. Their mother, Jessica, passed away from a heart attack.

The passing of his wife almost broke Gary. He was hurt and very distraught, feeling as if his life had been taken away from him. Despite his despair, he recognized that his daughters were young and in need of security and stability, now more than ever. He began to imagine what would happen to them if he didn't make it home one day. He loved his daughters deeply, and never wanted any harm to come to them.

But he realized in this moment that love was not enough to help them survive without their last living parent. He decided that life insurance would help bridge the gap and provide the stability they would need if he were to depart from this life prematurely. However, the task of buying a policy was difficult for Gary because he knew nothing about how life insurance worked.

So, he set out to find an insurance provider who would explain to him the entire process without trying to force a policy down his throat. Gary wanted to make the decision on his own. He just wanted the facts, the figures, and to understand the process so that he could make an informed decision.

He finally found an insurance agent he felt comfortable with, who enlightened him about a number of policies, and the benefits of each one. In the process of assessing Gary's needs, the agent began a line of questioning about what Gary deemed important. What he wanted to accomplish with the purchase of his life insurance policy? As Gary sat and pondered the question, his face lit up. He said, *"I saw an article about Life Diamonds. I would like each of my daughters to have a Life Diamond once I pass on."*

The agent had never heard of such a thing... so they proceeded to pull the item up online. It turned out that Life Diamonds are actual stones that are infused with the ashes of a deceased person after cremation. Gary wished to have diamond pendants made for each daughter to wear around her neck, infused with his ashes. The pendants were $7999 each. With the agent taking the time to do a thorough job, assessing Gary's needs properly, Gary's life insurance would now provide for something near and dear to his heart. That is what it is all about. Legacies are left in many forms. What type of legacy do you wish to leave behind you?

CHAPTER 4
WHAT IS AN ANNUITY?

The best way to describe an annuity is that it is a powerful financial planning tool. If this tool is used for the right situation at an appropriate time, it will be able to provide tremendous value to the annuity buyer. Buying an annuity will be able to give security and stability to an investor's portfolio, provided that it is used in an efficient manner. Unfortunately, a number of buyers misallocate their resources during the time of purchasing annuities. For this reason, they end up with an underperforming annuity that costs too much and pays too little.

This then results in the annuity being an inefficient use of their resources. An annuity can simply be explained as a contract between you and a third party, which is most likely an insurance company. It is a long-term, tax-deferred vehicle designed for retirement. Two major advantages of annuities are that the funds accumulate tax-deferred and they can be distributed in a variety of ways to the contract owner. The contract states that in exchange for making a lump sum payment, the insurance company will carry out a few things. These things are as follows:

- The insurance company will provide an income for a certain period of time, or for your entire life.
- It will be responsible for providing accumulation, or asset growth.
- It will provide a death benefit for the purchaser.
- It can also guarantee that you get long term care benefits.

Benefits:

- Predictable retirement income
- Tax-free growth
- No annual contribution limits
- Protection against outliving your savings
- Protection against losing your principal

Parties to an Annuity Contract

There are three parties to an annuity contract; the Owner, the Annuitant and the Beneficiary. In many instances, the Owner and Annuitant will be the same.

The Owner is usually the purchaser and has all the rights under the contract. The Owner names the Annuitant and the Beneficiary(ies). If the Owner dies while the contract is in the accumulation phase, there is a mandatory distribution of the death benefit.

The Annuitant must be a natural person and serves as the measuring life for purposes of determining the amount and duration of any annuity payments made under the contract.

The Beneficiary receives the death benefit or any remaining annuity payments upon the death of the owner.

There are many different types of annuities. Immediate annuities are designed to provide income right away, whereas deferred annuities are designed for long-term accumulation. Some annuities offer a guaranteed rate of interest, whereas others do not.

Annuities vs. CDs

Most people are familiar with Certificates of Deposits, more commonly known as CDs. Well an annuity functions somewhat like a CD, but with very distinctive differences. A Certificate of Deposit is a certificate issued by a bank to a person depositing money for a specified length of time. Those funds must stay in the bank for that selected length of time to earn a promised return. A CD is also called a *"share certificate"* at credit unions. An annuity works much like a certificate of deposit by guaranteeing a rate over a fixed period of time. However, with an annuity, the interest or gains are not taxed annually, but are allowed to grow tax-deferred until funds are withdrawn. With a CD, a 1099 is issued at year-end so that the owner can pay taxes on the gains. Annuities have early withdrawal and surrender provisions. The charge for doing so declines annually until the surrender period expires.

You have the flexibility of deciding exactly how much you want to withdraw. You don't have to surrender the entire annuity. With a CD, you must surrender the entire CD in order to retrieve any of your funds. In other words, you don't have the option of withdrawing $1000 from a $10,000 CD. You would have to surrender and pay a penalty on the entire $10,000 unless you specifically chose a Liquid CD.

Liquid CDs are similar to standard CDs, but they work more like traditional savings accounts in that they allow you to pull money out early. Your *"locked in"* period is relatively short with these CDs. This type of flexibility comes with a cost. You'll receive a lower interest rate in exchange for this freedom, somewhere in the neighborhood of 1.25 percent annually (in late 2018), while traditional CDs might pay around 1.7 percent, which tends to still be more than the average savings account. With most annuities, you can access up to 10% of your funds annually without penalty. This means that if you had $10,000 in your account, $1000 of your withdrawal would be penalty free.

Another major difference between a CD and an annuity is that an annuity can avoid probate, if the beneficiaries are set-up properly. An annuity policy does not *"mature"* like a Certificate of Deposit. Both the principal and interest will automatically continue to earn interest until withdrawn or age 100. You can let the money continue to grow, make withdrawals, or request an annuity income at any time.

Fixed Annuity

When you purchase a fixed annuity, the insurance company will guarantee you the minimum rate of interest along with the principal interest. It pays out a fixed rate of return on your money. It's a guaranteed, predictable income stream, no matter what's going on in the financial markets. Therefore, your principal amount will never drop in value, creating principal protection. The growth of the annuity's value and the benefits paid are determined by the issuing company. During the accumulation phase, the insurance company invests premiums in high-quality, fixed-income investments like bonds. The growth of the annuity's value and/or the benefits paid is not directly dependent on the investments that the insurance company makes to support the annuity.

Furthermore, some fixed annuities credit a higher interest rate than the minimum interest rate. This is done through a policy dividend. This dividend may be declared by the company's board of directors, if the condition is more favorable than was expected. These situations may occur when the company's actual investment, expense, and mortality experience is more than previously calculated.

Variable Annuity

Unlike fixed annuities, variable annuities provide irregular payments based on the performance of the underlying assets. Rather than investing in highly secure bonds and other debt securities, variable annuities generate income from a variety of specifically designed investment funds managed by the insurance company. Money in a variable annuity is invested in a fund. This fund operates like a mutual fund, but it is only open to investors in the insurance company's life insurance policies and various annuities. This fund has an investment objective which is very specific. The investment performance determines the value of your money in a variable annuity, as well as the amount of money to be paid out to you. Most variable annuities are designed so that they offer investors various fund alternatives.

This type of annuity is regulated by State Insurance Departments and the Federal Securities and Exchange Commission. In comparison to mutual funds, variable annuities have an advantage of a guaranteed death benefit feature. Irrespective of how the subaccounts perform, a variable annuity death benefit guarantees that the person who owns the annuity, their beneficiaries should receive an amount of money.

This sum should be greater than the initial investment. However, variable annuity investors are liable to pay for the cost of that protection by paying a mortality charge. Some variable annuities offer a minimum rate guarantee for an added charge, which will pay out the minimum rate of return even if the subaccounts experience a loss for the year. A similar option is offered for income payments at the time of annuitizing. This also guarantees a minimum payout rate irrespective of the performance of the subaccounts. Variable annuities can be considered as a long-term investment due to the limitations that are implemented on withdrawals. It is wise for investors to carefully read the terms and conditions of the contract and additional documents they are provided with. This will help them in gaining a full understanding of the expenses and risks. The expenses for a variable annuity can quickly add up.

These expenses can include an investment management fee, mortality fee, administrative fee and charges for any riders. If these charges are not taken into account at the time of signing up for an annuity, they can adversely affect returns over the long term. Variable annuities are generally the best option for experienced investors who have a little wiggle room in their finances.

As with any potentially volatile investment, the potential for profit is much larger than with the more stable fixed annuity, but so is the potential for loss. Variable annuities are sold by prospectus. Please consider the investment objectives, risks, charges, and expenses carefully before investing. The prospectus, which contains this and other information about the variable annuity contract and the underlying investment options, can be obtained from your financial professional. Be sure to read the prospectus carefully before deciding whether to invest.

Indexed Annuity

An indexed annuity pays out a rate of return on your money that's tied to an economic index, such as the S&P 500. It is considered a hybrid of the fixed and variable types because you receive a minimum guaranteed return, but can also enjoy a higher return when there are gains in the broader market. It is often said that the equity-indexed annuities give you the best of both worlds.

According to the Insured Retirement Institute's report, it credits a minimum guaranteed rate of interest over a fixed number of years, plus additional interest that may be credited based on the percentage change in the value of a broad market index. Insurers use participation rates, caps and spreads to limit the amount of interest that can be credited based on the change in value of the underlying stock market index.

By limiting the upside, the insurance company is able to purchase index options with the portion of the premium that is not invested at interest to support the minimum guaranteed interest rate. The indexed annuity now offers guaranteed lifetime withdrawal benefits which, The Insured Retirement Institute (IRI) says, makes them useful for saving for retirement as well as for income in retirement.

Immediate Vs. Deferred Payment

Most insurance companies offer two different payout options, immediate and deferred. An immediate annuity provides income right away—or at least within a year after you buy it. With immediate annuities, most often, the annuitant begins receiving income immediately after making a single lump sum investment called a single premium.

Payments can be made over a specific period, such as 10, 15, 20 years, or for the life of the annuitant, or for the life of the annuitant and their spouse (jointly). Often, this option is used by those who are already retired and need to generate regular income quickly. For example, let's say you receive a life insurance payment of one million dollars after taxes and you want to create a monthly income from investing that money into an annuity. At *immediateannuities.com* you can see what your monthly payment would be based on your age and gender. If you were a 40-year-old female, for instance, a $1,000,000 annuity would give you about $4,400 a month right now. A deferred annuity is one where you receive income at a future date. You make one or multiple contributions during the annuity's savings phase or *"accumulation phase"*, and then receive income either as periodic payments or as a lump sum during the *"distribution phase."* So, it's similar to a retirement account where you set aside money that you access in the future.

In fact, you can own a deferred annuity inside of a retirement account, such as a traditional IRA, 401(k), or 403(b). This annuity type is more common for younger investors who have time to let their investments grow. It defers payout, where the payout does not begin paying until a set date, usually at retirement. The benefit of deferred annuities is the fact that the investment accumulates earnings which are tax-free until those funds are withdrawn after retirement, much like with a 401(k), IRA, or 403(b).

Non-qualified Annuity

A non-qualified annuity is one that's owned outside of a retirement account. With a non-qualified annuity, you must contribute after-tax dollars. There are no annual contribution limits, so you can put in as much money as you like. Even though you've paid taxes on your contributions to a non-qualified annuity up front, you defer paying taxes on the earnings until you take withdrawals after the age of 59½. However, your principal payments are paid tax-free because you have already paid taxes on those funds. Unlike a qualified annuity that's held inside of a retirement account, you don't have to start taking distributions at any particular age.

Qualified Annuity

In a qualified annuity you invest and disburse money in a tax-favored retirement plan. This plan could be an IRA or other similar plan, which are laid out by Internal Revenue Code sections, 401(k), 403(b), or 457. In accordance with these terms of the plan, money paid into the annuity which are the premiums or contributions, does not fall into taxable income for the year in which it is paid into the qualified plan. In addition to that, all other tax provisions that can be applied to non-qualified annuities are also applicable to qualified annuities. If you own an annuity inside of a retirement account it's called a qualified annuity and its subject to traditional retirement account rules in the fact that you contribute pre-tax dollars, which are subject to the annual limit set forth by the IRS.

These limits are subject to change. Make certain that you check the limits for the applicable year in which you make contributions. Not only can you deduct your contributions from your taxable income in most cases, but you also defer paying taxes on the annuity's earnings each year. You pay taxes on the money when you make withdrawals after the age 59½ years. With a qualified annuity you must begin taking distributions no later than age of 70½ years.

How Are Traditional and Roth IRA Accounts Different?

An Individual Retirement Account (IRA) is a personal retirement savings plan available to anyone who receives taxable compensation during the year. For IRA contribution purposes, compensation includes wages, salaries, fees, tips, bonuses, commissions, taxable alimony, self-employment income, and separate maintenance payments. You or your spouse must have earned income to be eligible for contributing to Traditional and Roth IRAs. Before you determine your eligibility to deduct your Traditional IRA contribution or to make Roth IRA contributions, note some of the differences between the two.

Traditional IRAs

Traditional IRAs are best when you are in your prime money-making years and can make good use of tax deductions. They are especially appealing to employees who want to save for retirement but don't have retirement plans at work. However, many people have both a 401(k) and an IRA. Typically, they contribute to their IRAs after they have contributed enough money into their 401(k)s to get their employer match.

- Contributions may be tax-deductible, but distributions are generally taxable
- Often, contributions are 100 percent deductible
- Earnings grow tax-deferred
- Distributions are generally taxable, but are penalty free if distributed under one of the following circumstances:
  - attaining age 59 1/2
  - incurring a disability
  - paying for certain health insurance, medical expenses, and higher education expenses
  - paying first-time homebuyer expenses
  - taking equal, periodic payments
  - satisfying an IRS tax levy
  - being a qualified reservist
  - death (payments to beneficiaries)
- Distributions are required to be taken by Traditional IRA holders beginning at age 70 ½

Roth IRAs

With Roth IRAs, contributions are not deductible, but distributions generally can be distributed tax free. It has annual income and contribution limits.

- Contributions are not tax deductible
- Earnings can grow tax free
- Contributions can generally be distributed tax free at any time
- Earnings can be distributed tax free if the Roth IRA holder first made a Roth IRA contribution at least five years ago, AND one of the following events occurs:
  - attaining age 59 ½
  - incurring a disability
  - incurring first time homebuyer expenses
  - death (payments to beneficiaries)
- Distributions are not required by Roth IRA holders, though beneficiaries may be subject to required distributions

Simplified Employee Pension (SEP) Plan

A SEP provides business owners with a simplified method to contribute toward their employees' retirement as well as to their own retirement savings. Contributions are made to an Individual Retirement Account or Annuity (IRA) set up for each plan participant.

Income for Life

Would you like to have peace of mind in knowing that you won't outlive your income? Wouldn't you like to know that your income is guaranteed until you part from this life? An annuity can do this for you. Your annuity income is calculated at the time you buy the annuity. It's based on a number of factors. The most important ones are interest rates and your life expectancy.

Factors

Current interest rates

If interest rates are high when you buy your annuity, your annuity payments will be higher than if interest rates were lower.

The amount you deposit

The more money you put into your annuity, the more you get back as income.

Your age

The older you are when you purchase the annuity, the higher your annuity payments will be. That's because you're not expected to live as long as the term of the annuity.

Your gender

Women get less money than men of the same age because they are expected to live longer.

The length of time the payments are guaranteed

You choose the number of years you receive payments; the shorter the term, the higher the payments. If you have a life annuity, you can arrange for your annuity payments to continue to your spouse, your dependent children, or your estate after you die. The longer you want payments to continue after your death, the less you get each month while you're alive.

The options you add

You get the highest income with a basic annuity that covers only you. Any options you add, such as a joint-and-last survivor option, will lower the amount of your payments. These extras increase the costs to the insurance company.

In the event the Owner should die during the deferred/accumulation phase of the contract, a distribution to the surviving owner or beneficiary is mandatory. They may select one of the applicable payment options:

- Immediate lump sum
- Complete withdrawal within 5 years of death
- Annuitizing based on the life of the new owner to begin within one year
- If the spouse is the sole surviving owner or beneficiary, he/she can elect to continue the contract
- If Owner is a grantor trust, death triggers a mandatory distribution.

Tax Shelters

Many investments are taxed year by year, but the investment earnings, or capital gains, and investment income in annuities aren't taxable until you withdraw money. This tax deferral is also true of 401(k)s and IRAs; however, unlike these financial products, there are no limits on the amount you can put into an annuity. Moreover, the minimum withdrawal requirements for annuities are much more liberal than they are for 401(k)s and IRAs. Withdrawals of annuity earnings are taxed as ordinary income and may be subject to surrender charges, plus a 10 percent federal income tax penalty if made prior to age 59½. Tax-deferred annuities are safe. A qualified legal reserve life insurance company is required to meet its contractual obligations. These reserves must, at all times, be equal to the withdrawal value of the annuity policy. In addition to reserves, the state law also requires certain levels of capital and surplus to further increase policyholder protection. Legal reserve refers to the strict financial requirements that must be met by an insurance company to protect the money paid in by all policyholders.

Protection from Creditors

If you own an immediate annuity and you are receiving money from an insurance company, generally the most that creditors can access are the payments as they're made to you, since the money you gave the insurance company now belongs to the company. Some state statutes and court decisions also protect some or all of the payments made to you from annuities. In addition, your money in tax-favored retirement plans, such as IRAs and 401(k)s, is generally protected, whether invested in an annuity or not.

Benefits to Your Heirs

There is a common misconception about annuities that if you start an immediate lifetime annuity and die soon after that, the insurance company keeps all of your investment in the annuity. That can happen, but it doesn't have to. To prevent it, buy a *"guaranteed period"* with the immediate annuity.

A guaranteed period commits the insurance company to continue payments after you die to one or more beneficiaries you designate. The payments continue to the end of the stated guaranteed period which is usually 10 or 20 years. This time is measured from when you started receiving annuity payments. Furthermore, annuity benefits that pass to beneficiaries don't go through probate and are not governed by your Will.

Annuity Story

This story references one of the most famous cases in recent American history. This is the case of a person who was accused of murdering his wife and his wife's boyfriend. After a long and highly publicized trial that lasted more than eight months with attorney fees accumulating to approximately $5 million, says the LA Times; after 54 witnesses listed for the defense, and 72 for the prosecution were heard, the accused was acquitted. Even though the accused was declared not guilty by a jury, this did not sit well with the victim's family. The family of the male victim decided to pursue this famous person in civil court for the damages they felt he had caused them.

They did prevail in court and they were awarded a civil judgment of $33.5 million. The prevailing family was not paid then and has not received one payment to date, despite the fact that Mr. Famous is receiving a pension of over $20,000 per month. In addition, Mr. Famous' remaining assets are also in the form of annuities. Therefore, his income and assets fall under the safe umbrella the protection from creditors that the annuity provides. An insurance contract saved him from destitution!

CHAPTER 5
WHAT IS PROBATE? HOW TO AVOID IT?

The process of legally distributing a deceased person's estate correctly among their heirs and designated beneficiaries is known as Probate. Any debt owed to their creditors is also paid off through this process. The distribution of the probate property happens as per the deceased person's last Will and testament if there is any. Otherwise, the decedent's property is distributed in accordance with the state law. The probate process involves locating and determining the value of the deceased person's assets.

In addition to paying off the debts owed by the deceased person, this process includes paying their final bills and taxes. After this, the remainder of their estate and possessions are distributed to their rightful heirs and/or beneficiaries. Unfortunately, this process is often arduous to follow because most people don't leave behind a Will. If you do not have a written Will at the time of your death, then the court and an appointed administrator decides how your estate is distributed among your heirs. It is not wise to assume that your spouse or your children will get all of your possessions and assets. In fact, the court may have difficulty distributing your assets equally among your heirs in the absence of a Will. One of the primary reasons for such inconveniences is the fact that each state has a different set of laws. Every state has a different temperament when it comes to the distribution of property after death. These laws are known as *"probate codes."*

When a person passes away without writing a Will, the statue is known as **intestate succession**. Simply stated, the person dies intestate (without a Will). The purpose of the intestate succession is to distribute the decedent's property in an organized and methodical manner. The law changes from state to state. However, some steps in the probate process stay consistent across the board. The following procedures remain the same:

- If the decedent has left a Will behind, the judge will need to confirm its authenticity, and the time it was compiled. If it is in fact, the most recent valid Will signed by the deceased, the property will be distributed as per the Will.
- The judge appoints a personal representative to represent the deceased. The representative can also be referred to as an executor or administrator. The administrator oversees the probate process and takes steps to settle the estate. The Will typically include the decedent's choice for an executor. However, when there is no Will, the court usually appoints next of kin as administrator.
- The personal representative will then have to locate and protect all of the decedent's assets.
- The personal representative determines the values of the decedent's assets as on the date of death. This is done by going through account statements and appraisals of the property owned by the deceased.
- The personal representative verifies all of the decedent's creditors and notifies them of the death. The representative may also need to publish a notice of the deceased's death in a local newspaper to alert the creditors of the deceased individual's death so they can make contact with the representative. Although the creditors are given an opportunity to collect monies owed, the window is limited. They can only make claims within a specified time frame against the estate for the monies they're owed. Therefore, this process needs haste and should be handled expeditiously.
- It is the job of the personal representative to pay the decedent's final bills which also include claims by creditors. The representative also has the authority to reject claims if he/she has reason to believe that they are invalid. In this scenario, the creditor might then petition the court so that a probate judge can decide whether the claim should be paid or not.
- The personal representative also files the decedent's final personal income tax returns. Besides, that person will determine if the estate is liable to pay any inheritance taxes. If

the estate is indeed liable, then these tax returns must also be filed. The representative will pay any taxes that are due from the estate funds even if it requires liquidating assets in some cases. These taxes have a due date of nine months from the decedent's date of death which the representative will adhere to strictly.

- After the completion of these steps, the personal representative can then petition the court for permission to distribute the remainder of the decedent's assets. The remaining assets will be distributed in accordance with the Will among the beneficiaries mentioned in the document. If there is no Will, the probate judge will decide how assets are distributed.

Problems with Probate

The probate process is imperative, but not easy. It comes with many issues. The following problems with probate may arise. You should be aware of them in order to resolve them quickly.

High Cost

It is not a free system. Even when the courts are working with a valid Will, there are costs and fees associated with the process that is paid to the courts, and other businesses related to the process. If there is no Will, or its validity is in question, the costs to help administer the estate will be higher than usual. Probate and administrative fees have the capacity of taking 6% to 10% of a person's total estate value. This does not include any deductions or liens that may be owed in taxes, or other debts.

Excessive Time

Probate takes a long time to finalize. Therefore, it is not wise for you to depend on the assets of the estate to make arrangements for the burial of the deceased. In addition, immediate needs such as the payment for the mortgage, college tuition, medical bills, or other items that are time-sensitive may also be a matter of concern to some people. Not to mention, the probate process has many expenses. The excessive time involved in this process may cause many difficulties for you. You must have some financial back up that is not aligned with the estate of the deceased.

The expenses of the probate process can be extensive. For instance, real estate is an asset that may be involved in the Will. If so, you will need to pay its mortgage(s), along with taxes and homeowners' insurance, even in cases where no one is living in the home. The cost of the probate process and the amount of the home's expenses will vary. Therefore, the cost could add up steeply. The usual time frame required for the settlement of an estate is from nine months to two years. If the estate is disputed, or the workings of the settlement are complex, then it could take much longer. This will result in the heirs having to wait until probate is concluded to receive a significant part of their inheritance. By that point, there is a chance that the estate may have exhausted itself merely to cover its expenses. You must try to complete the probate process as soon as possible in order to avoid delays and extra expenses.

Family Disagreements

The probate process slows down considerably when family disagreements arise. There are many families holding grudges against each other because of inheritance issues. Such problems usually erupt after the death of a family member and when his/her heirs are inline to collect their inherited assets. It especially becomes more difficult when there are families that have been blended due to marriage and divorce, or when the deceased has a large fortune.

There may also be mounting issues when the family members of the deceased person do not like or trust the person that has been chosen as the executor of the estate, In the probate process, anyone can contest the contents of a Will. If that happens, your heirs will have to hire lawyers to go through the court system to resolve the dispute legally. At this point, a judge would appoint an administrator. The administrator and the judge will meet with the attorneys to discover who has a valid claim. If the claim proves to be valid, then like in any other court proceeding, the claimants will need to produce evidence, witnesses, and testimonies. This process will consume additional time and money. Furthermore, if there is any salacious material revealed, there is a massive chance that the family feud will be publicized. All types of secrets and undiscussed family business could become available for public display. Such disagreements are quite common, and if they exist in your case, you must act on resolving them as quickly as possible.

No Security for the Information Shared

There is no privacy of information because the probate courts are a matter of public record. Anyone who desires to look into your wealth can go to the courthouse to find out particular details. These details can include expenses that were made in the courts, your tax history, and most importantly exactly how much you left each heir, or to whom, you owed money. This matter is not limited to large estates. Anyone with any amount of inheritance can have their financial status scrutinized. It gives way to a begrudged ex, or to a real estate investor interested in your property to create troubles for the actual inheritors.

Pets

For the purpose of inheriting, pets are also considered property. Just like any of your other possessions, your cat, dog, horse or any other pet will be considered for inheritance. With naming the people who would be responsible for caring for your pets in your Will, you would be saving the pets and their inheritor a lot of trouble.

You can create trusts for your pets in which you can also establish the way you want the custodian of your pet to take care of them in your Last Will and Testament. However, these trusts are separate from the ones that have been set by you for your family. But some trusts do offer support for pets so take that into consideration when setting them up.

Legal Foundation

Assets that bypass probate are life insurance policies, IRAs, pension plans, personal annuities, buy/sell agreements and smaller estates. The most significant amongst all these exceptions is the possession of a smaller estate. This is because some states have laws that exempt them from being in the probate system while some other states expedite the process of a smaller estate. For example, the set amount for such estates must not exceed $30,000 in New York to qualify for a summarized probate hearing. Others may allow affidavits to be presented to claim property. You have to determine the legal foundation of your probate before you begin your process. In the case of the above-mentioned assets, you can avoid the probate process altogether. Due to the difficulties in this process, it is wise to avoid it where you can.

To understand the legalities concerning your estate, you can run a simple search on Google with the name of your state and the words *"probate process"* accompanying it. It is essential that you take your information from a state website that has been recently updated. Be careful that you are not looking at a web search result that is outdated. It is also wise to verify the information with an attorney in order to be sure. You can also call the probate court for this matter.

When an asset is jointly owned by a spouse, it can usually avoid probate. For example, the home that is owned by you and your spouse can skip probate if, God forbid, one of you passes away. If both names are on the title of the deed, then it's accepted as joint property. Another example is the joint checking and savings account. In these cases, the way the asset is titled is fundamental. The rule states that possession is jointly owned if more than one person is on the title of the asset. In this case, it may be able to avoid the probate process. Please note that just because you are married to someone, does not guarantee that your spouse's property will pass directly to you when he or she passes away. It is contingent on the law in your state.

For instance, if a case was handled in a particular way in Minnesota, it does not mean it will happen the same way in Arizona. This is why it is necessary to get legal advice from an attorney. An attorney will provide you with proper guidance in accordance with your state's law. Some other possessions to consider are things such as cash, homes, boats, investment accounts, jewelry, etc.

If these are owned by a single person, then usually a surviving spouse must pass through probate. But the process can be avoided if a trust is set up by the deceased before his/her death. If you have set up a trust, then it will enable you to pass your estate on to your heirs without them going through probate. People assume that trusts are only required for rich people so that they can pass their wealth down to their children when they turn 18 years old.

However, a person with an average income may also have assets that need to be passed down to their heirs, which is why it is a useful option for any middle-class family. In a trust, the trustee is the legal guardian of the assets which are considered the property of the trust that you chose. It can own anything that is tangible which ranges from real estate, vehicles, bank accounts, to investments that you've made.

Just like a life insurance policy, the trust also has a beneficiary. To set up a trust, you must work with an attorney. Avoid using off-the-shelf forms for this purpose. Although there are costs linked to setting up your trust, the amount you spend will be less expensive than setting up your trust incorrectly, or not having one at all. The cost to open a trust can vary from $500 to more than $2,000. It all depends on the property you own, the kind of trust you require, and the number of assets you have.

WILLs

As a legal document, a Will establishes your wishes with regard to the distribution of your property. It also specifies the care of any minor children. For a greater chance that your wishes are carried out, you should have a Will in writing and signed. In the case your Will does not meet standard requirements, your instructions will not be carried out. There are various types of Wills:

Self-Proving Will

A self-proving Will is also known as a testamentary Will. It is the traditional type of Will. Many people are familiar with it. It is a formally prepared document which is signed in the presence of witnesses. A Will has a legal substance that is used to transfer an estate to its beneficiaries. Testamentary Wills appoint guardians for minor children and select executors of the Will. They are also used for creating trusts. Any person over who is of the age of majority and of sound mind can draft a Will.

Holographic Will

There are no witnesses present when Holographic Wills are written. They rarely hold up in court. A holographic Will is a handwritten; testator signed document and is an alternative to a Will produced by a lawyer. Some states do not recognize holographic Wills. States that do permit holographic Wills require that the documented Will meet specific requirements to stay valid. The minimal requirements for most states are proof the Will was written by a testator who had the mental capacity to write it. The Will must contain the testator's wish for disbursing personal property to beneficiaries.

Oral Will

Oral Wills are spoken before witnesses. They are not legal in many states. An oral Will is made verbally to others and with the intent of carrying out the wishes of the dying individual.

Living Will

A Living Will does not distribute assets but instead establishes your wishes for medical care in the case that you are incapacitated. A Living Will is an advance directive, a legal document which specifies the medical care that an individual does or does not want in the event that he or she is incapable of communicating his or her needs.

For an unconscious person, who is suffering from a terminal illness or a life-threatening injury, doctors, and hospitals defer to his or her living Will to identify whether or not the patient wants treatment to sustain their life, such as assisted breathing, or feeding from a tube. Without a living Will, decisions regarding medical care becomes the primary responsibility of your spouse, family members, or other parties responsible for your care. Sometimes such individuals may be unaware of the patient's desires, or they may not wish to follow the patient's unwritten, verbal directives.

> ➢ *Health Proxy*
>
> A health care proxy identifies someone that you can rely on as your proxy, or agent, to express your wishes and make health care decisions for you if you cannot speak for yourself. A proxy ensures that you get the health care you prefer in the event that you cannot communicate your wishes.

Why Do You Need Wills?

Creating a Will gives you authority over the distribution of your assets after your death. It lets you decide how your possessions are distributed after you are no longer in this world. Your Will can direct the transition of assets related to your business and investments. A Will allows you to provide care for your minor children. Your Will can even dictate the assets that your married children receive. Creating a Will minimizes tension among survivors over property disputes. In case you want to give to charity, a Will also provide you with options for donating your estate. Likewise, if you intend to leave your assets to an institution or organization, a Will can fulfill your intentions with ease.

What Does a Will NOT Contain?

While Wills address the bulk of your assets, there are many items not covered by instructions described in a Will. Such items include community property, proceeds from life insurance policy payouts, assets retained through retirement, assets owned as joint tenants that have rights of survivorship, and investment accounts that are designated to *"transfer on death."*

What Happens If You Don't Prepare a Will?

If you do not create a Will, you die intestate (without a Will). In the case of intestate death, the state will take care of the distribution of the assets you own. The state does not inherit your assets; rather it distributes them according to a set formula. This formula often gives half your estate to your spouse and the other half going to your children. Such a scenario can result in the forced sale of the family home or other assets, negatively affecting the surviving spouse. This can create financial and emotional difficulties, mainly if your spouse depended on the bulk of your assets for maintaining his or her standard of living. Further complications may arise if your children are minors, as the court will appoint a representative to look after their interests.

Tax considerations are another critical issue that must be considered, and a Will can reduce tax liability. People who have a large estate can take great benefit from this. In the U.S., an estate tax return must be filed on estates which are valued at $5,450,000 or more (as of 2016). However, but no federal estate tax is due if the estate is worth less than that amount.

When you are ready to have your Will prepared, you should compile a list of your assets and debts. You must include the contents of your safe deposit boxes, items of sentimental value, heirlooms and various other assets that you wish to transfer to a particular person or entity. If your estate is substantial (comprising of millions of dollars) or your situation is legally complicated, you must enlist the help of an attorney. Try to work with someone who is familiar with your state's laws and has extensive experience in preparing Wills. Your state bar association may be able to help you in locating a suitable attorney. However, if you are comfortable in taking care of the task on your own, there are software programs available to assist you, as well as a variety of websites.

How Can You Change Your Will?

Changing your Will is easy. Just write a new Will to replace the old one, or make an addition using an amendment known as a codicil. Ideally, you would want to make any changes to your will when you are of sound mind and in good health. This limits the likelihood of your wishes being successfully challenged, and it avoids decisions being made in haste or under intense emotional pressure.

What Do You Do with Your Will Once It Is Prepared?

Once prepared you have to hand over your Will to your executor or professional advisor. Remember that your wishes can only be carried out if they are known. Placing your Will in capable hands ensures that it will be available when it is needed.

The Bottom Line

A Will is a necessary document and a relatively simple one. It can save your family time, money and grief. It also gives you peace of mind.

TRUSTs

A trust fund is a legal entity that holds property for the benefit of another person, group, or organization. . Once you hold assets in the trust, they do not belong to you. They go under the care of a trustee. A trustee is a bank, attorney, or other entity set up for this purpose. As the assets are no longer yours, you don't have to pay income tax on any money made from the assets. A trust is created for a beneficiary who is entitled to its benefits (such as assets, income, etc.).

The fund can have nearly any asset imaginable, such as cash, stocks, bonds, property, or other types of financial assets. Among the chief advantages of trusts, the biggest one is that they let you put conditions on how and when your assets are to be distributed after you die, reduce taxes, and distribute assets to heirs efficiently without the cost, delay, and publicity of probate court. Wills and Trusts are estate planning documents designed to pass assets on to beneficiaries at death.

However, there are distinct advantages of using a Trust instead of a Will. Below are five ways in which a Trust works much more efficiently:

A Trust is Used to Avoid Probate – a Will cannot

In probate, the title on asset changes when the person who owns it passes away. Assets owned in the name of the deceased person are inaccessible for all of their successors. If family members want to get access to accounts or other assets in the deceased individual's name, they must file a request with the probate court and wait for the court to approve the Will and appoint a Personal Representative to carry out the process of probate.

Probate is a long and costly process during which bills are not paid, and assets are not managed well. A Trust is an excellent probate avoidance tool because assets that are owned in the name of a Trust are immediately accessible to the appointed successor of the trust maker.

A Trust can Give Creditor Protection for the Inheritance Left to Beneficiaries – a Will cannot

Many people worry that the inheritance they leave to their children will be lost to their children's creditors such as a divorcing spouse, unpaid credit card bills, a bankruptcy, a business loss, or a lawsuit. Sadly, this is often the case when assets are distributed to beneficiaries via a Will. A Trust allows the maker to safeguard an inheritance from the reach of the beneficiaries' creditors by keeping the assets out of the name of the beneficiary.

Ownership of the assets remains in the Trust. The beneficiary will have access to the assets in accordance with the directions you leave in the Trust. You may also allow your beneficiary to serve as Trustee, allowing the beneficiary to manage their own inheritance. By leaving assets to your beneficiaries via a Trust rather than outright via your Will, you can ensure that the assets you worked so hard for will be available to your heirs.

A Trust can Protect Governmental Benefits for a Person with Disabilities – a Will cannot

If you have a child, grandchild or other beneficiaries with disabilities, then you must create a Trust. If you leave assets to a person who receives needs-based governmental benefits via your Will, it will place your beneficiary in a difficult position of either losing those benefits or transferring inheritance to a Trust that has the state as a beneficiary in case the actual beneficiary dies.

Unless the inheritance you are leaving is so significant that the monetary and medical benefits available to the person through programs such as Social Security and Medicaid are no longer relevant, then ensuring that benefits given by the government continue to be available is vital. Leaving assets to a person with disabilities via a Trust is the best way to ensure that those government benefits continue and that the inheritance you are leaving will be able to pay for expenses that are not covered by such benefits.

Trusts can Reduce Estate Taxes – a Traditional Will cannot

Many married couples have so-called *"I-love-you"* Wills, which leave all assets outright to the surviving spouse upon the first death. If you have an estate of more than $1,000,000, then using *"I-love-you"* Wills means that the money you think you are leaving to your beneficiaries will, in fact, be going to the Commonwealth of your respective state in the form of estate tax payable at the surviving spouse's death. Estate tax planning via Trusts for married couples is standard planning and permissible under both state and federal tax laws.

A Trust can Administer Assets for Minor Beneficiaries without Court Intervention – a Will cannot.

Leaving money directly to a minor creates an administrative nightmare because the law provides that a minor does not have the legal capacity to receive assets. The parent of the minor also does not have the ability to act as the child's legal representative until the court says so. As such, if you die with a Will that leaves money to minor beneficiaries, the court will need to appoint a Conservator to receive that inheritance for the minor. The Conservator will be required to report annually to the court, and the court will appoint an overseer (guardian ad litem) to make sure the Conservator is doing his or her job for the minor beneficiaries. This means enormous costs and long delays in administering funds for minors. It also means that when the minor turns 18 years old, he or she will be entitled to receive all those assets and will be free to do with them as he or she wishes (think fast cars, spring break, and lots of shopping).

Creating a Trust to receive assets passing to a minor, or even to a young adult beneficiary, is the best way to ensure that the court is not involved in the process, that the person you want to manage assets for the beneficiary is able to do so, and that the beneficiary can use the assets only for purposes you decide are necessary and/or at ages that you dictate.

These are just five ways in which a Trust is superior to a Will. If you want to know more about whether a Trust is right for your situation, contact an experienced estate planner to discuss your goals.

Attorney Suzanne R. Sayward is certified as an Elder Law Attorney by the National Elder Law Foundation. She is a partner with the Dedham firm of Samuel, Sayward & Baler LLC. This article is not intended to provide legal advice or create or imply an attorney-client relationship. No information contained herein is a substitute for a personal consultation with an attorney. For more information visit www.ssbllc.com **or call 781/461-1020.** *May 2017 © 2017 Samuel, Sayward & Baler LLC*

Cost Variance between Legal Documents vs. Probate Costs

When you set up a trust, you get to decide who gets what. You are able to decide when a person receives a particular possession. You can set stipulations such as your heir may not be granted their inheritance until they turn 21 years of age. You are also able to decide how that person is going to receive the said possession.

It means that you can give your possessions outright, or in different types of trusts that offer a variety of protections. When you pass away, your family and friends will not be burdened with the task of going through probate to transfer title. The trustee who you've named in your trust will be required to go to an attorney. The attorney should be one who has specialized in this field. They will then have to start trust administration which generally consists of:

- Providing notice to the beneficiaries informing them that after you have passed away, the Successor Trustee is going to oversee the assets that are transitioned to the beneficiaries.
- Helping to update the title deed to your real estate, cars, finances and the like.
- Preparing tax forms and paying money due to creditors.
- Distribution of assets, and if specified, opening sub-trusts.

In instances where there are no complications, the process can take between 4 to 6 months. The distribution of the assets can be made prior to the closing of the trust most often. Unlike in the case of probate, the cost is not set by law. Instead, the attorney gets paid his hourly rate. The successor Trustee is also only entitled to 1% of the assets of the deceased for one year of work.

The total amount accumulates to significantly less than the fee associated with probate. Unlike a Will, which is only triggered when you have died, a trust can also protect you when you are incapacitated. This means that if you are physically or mentally disabled, your successor trustee can declare to manage your assets and care for you. But, just like any other policy, there are a few drawbacks that you must be aware of. In the case of a Will, when it has been drafted and signed by you in the presence of witnesses, your work is complete. Whereas, when a trust is drafted, signed, and duly notarized, there are still some requirements that need to be met. There are a few adjustments that need to be made.

You would be required to change the title to your property to the actual name of the estate.

That is how it will pass on to the trust; however, the trust will help you in carrying out this task along with your attorney. Similarly, you will also need to change the title to your bank accounts. You will have to do this task on your own. Any other assets that you wish to place in the trust should have a name change to the trust's title as well.

Just because the trust mentions specific assets in the contract, it doesn't mean that they are in the trust. You are required to change the title of those assets. If you had some assets that weren't titled as trust assets, for example, you missed changing the title of a bank account, and it is included in the Will. The *"Will"* is able to direct the Judge to look to the Trust to determine where the assets should go and merely acts as a guidance tool.

When you have a Trust, there is no need for probate, and thus you do not require court supervision. However, there are still some costs that you may have to incur in the distribution of your trust. The most prominent of these expenses are the successor trustee fees. They are either dictated by the terms of the trust agreement or could be determined by state law. These laws help in maintaining a guideline which will be used to determine what is considered a reasonable fee. This fee is based on how complex the trust is, the amount of time it will take to administer and settle the trust, and whether the estate is subject to estate taxes.

Accounting fees also play a part in the trust expenses. It depends on the entire value of the trust and the kinds of assets it possesses. A small trust which may own 25 different stocks and bonds will have a particular value. These stocks may generate more in the way of accounting fees. In comparison, a more substantial trust may possess fewer items which include a primary residence, a bank account, and an automobile of average market value. If the grantor's estate is subject to taxes in respect of the estate at the state or federal level, the accounting fees can vary immensely. It will include the preparation and filing of the tax returns, which will make the costs climb higher. As of 2016, the federal estate tax exemption is $5.45 million. However, state thresholds are often significantly less. Even estates that do not owe taxes or require a return at the federal level are still required to deal with this expenditure at the state level. In addition, appraisal and business evaluation fees will also be required to determine the date of death values of real estate. Additional items could be anything ranging from jewelry, antiques, artwork, boats, and cars. Furthermore, business interests held by the trust must also be evaluated and considered. Appraisal fees for personal property can range anywhere from a few hundred to a few thousand dollars, while business evaluation fees will typically run several thousand dollars.

The Probate Timeline

The probate process, on an average, is completed six to nine months in the court. This timeline can vary depending on the court. It may also take years if there are disputes over the legal status of the Will or distribution of assets. There may also be costs linked to the probate process (such as court fees), a responsibility that the executor of the decedent's Will has to cater if they cannot be paid by the estate.

Steps	Duration
Prepare and File Petition for Probate	1-2 months
A court hearing on the Petition for Probate	2-3 months
Issued: Letters of Administration, Orders for Probate, Duties & Liabilities, Issue Bond (if ordered), & Letters of Testamentary	2-4 months (if not contested)
Notice to Creditors	2-4 months
Estate Inventory & Appraisement	4-8 months
Pay State and Federal Taxes (if necessary)	6-12 months
Allow or Reject Creditor Claims	-
Possible Preliminary Distributions	-
Notice to Department of Health Services (if deceased received medical)	-
Notice to Franchise Tax Board	-
The claim of Exemption (if assets transfer to a minor)	6-15 months
Receive Final Tax Letter from State and Federal (if appropriate)	6-18 months

File Petition for Final Distribution & Accounting	8-16 months
Hearing on Petition for final Distribution & Accounting	-
Order Approving Final Distribution & Accounting	-
Distribution of Assets to Heirs	9-17 months
Final Discharge Order (indicates close of probate case)	9-18 months
Final Distribution of Estate Funds (probate concluded)	9-18 months

CHAPTER 6
THE BENEFITS OF HAVING A FINANCIAL COUNSELOR

Planning

Financial planning can merely be described as wisely managing your money. Planning helps you in dealing with financial pitfalls that inevitably arise in various stages of life. Management of your personal finances is surely your personal responsibility. But that does not mean that you have to do it all alone.

A qualified financial planner, representative, coach, strategist, or counselor can help you make the decisions that enable you to be better at managing your finances. There are multiple reasons why you should consider having a financial partner to assist you with mapping out your finances:

- To help you with setting goals that are realistic, achievable, and in sync with your overall mission.
- To help you with analyzing your financial health, where you currently stand financially. To do so, there is an examination of your investments, assets, taxes, incomes, liabilities, insurance and estate plans.
- Addressing financial weaknesses through a better understanding of your resources, and to also build on your financial strengths.
- To assist you with carrying out your current and monitoring its progress.
- Staying updated on your finances will allow you to prepare for anything, giving you the opportunity to shape your goals accordingly.

Not everyone will need a financial partner. Some people possess the ability to manage their finances better than anyone else. Yet there are still many people who require financial assistance. This may be because they have a purpose in their journey and they intend to achieve their goal through better counsel on money matters.

A financial advisor is up to date with current market conditions and can offer multiple approaches to a singular goal through his/her experience. There are times when the steps needed to be taken are either emotionally challenging or physically tough, especially when it comes to cutting expenses.

A third-party perspective on these difficult decisions tends to help people make better choices in life. A financial partner will not only provide you with ways to save money, but also provides a sense of accountability. Financial planning will enable you to stay focused and follow through with your financial plans much more effectively. There are many circumstances that can trigger a person to avail the services of a financial professional. One of the most common reasons that people choose to begin a financial plan is because of marriage.

The second is because of the birth of a child. Some other reasons include saving money for retirement, facing a crisis such as an illness that has been going on for a long time, even the death of a loved one can prompt some people to get serious about their finances. The death of a loved one can also trigger an inheritance being passed through (a large sum of money or assets from a deceased person). It would be a good idea to make sure that a professional is in place to assist heirs with managing this new money. You would want to avoid the pitfalls that occur when people are thrust into a new asset level, handling sums of money that they have no prior experience managing.

Experience

When choosing a financial partner, you must employ a person who can be trusted. It is best that you look up the prospective representative's credentials. Check out their background, ask people who have used their services, interview them to see if you can find a sense of comfort with them. Just like your lawyers, your financial advisors are your representatives as well.

In order to be more careful of who to trust with your finances, you can look at a few aspects of their business methods. Here is how to know if your financial counselor is looking out for your best interest or just his own interests. They must ask you about your personal goals and your preferred time frame in which you want to achieve the said goals. These are the types of things they should be asking before recommending investments or any other products to you. There must be an interview process. They should get details about your current situation, as well as your future aspirations.

One-size-fits-all financial plans do not exist because everyone's finances, goals, and time horizons are different. In addition, everyone has their own tolerance for risk. In order for your financial partner to fully understand your finances, there is some initial groundwork to be done. You should always receive a written financial plan, prospectus, illustration, or some type of documentation from your counselor. A detailed written description can help you in understanding your direction better. You should have documentation that addresses your personal financial situation, and that outlines a financial road map to reach your goals, whether short term or long term.

Peace of Mind

Working with a financial partner/counselor will give you a greater sense of peace. You will find peace of mind in knowing that you are moving in the right direction because your progression will be tracked. Having a professional on your team gives you access to tools and advisement that could provide greater security when you are making decisions regarding life-changing events. You will find yourself making different decisions as to what you want to do with additional dollars that come your way.

Watching your finances will motivate you to do more. Once you turn a certain corner, reach a particular horizon, it will be so liberating for you. When you come across unexpected money, you may find yourself torn between whether you should splurge or save. You may become more driven to reduce debt.

Your counselor could help you in developing plans to accomplish this. The most commonly targeted loans are student loan debt, auto, and home loans. Until these loans are paid off, you are burdened with the responsibility of making timely payments or risk your creditworthiness. I am sure you would agree that just like good physical health, positive financial health can sure help you sleep at night.

Preventative Care

Maintenance and regular checkups are necessary components of a solid financial plan. Adding structure and balance to your budget is an absolute must. This can also be described as financial allocation and spreading costs. Diversifying investments is another essential component. Diversification will help in reducing the risk of your entire portfolio declining if one of the markets fall. While diversification in investments can help reduce the risk of losing too much, not all risk is investment specific. There are times when things just do not go as planned. Holistic financial planning focuses on other aspects of your financial life, not just pure investments. Finances like retirement planning, tax planning, estate planning, insurance, and debt reduction should also be areas of focus. Since every person's situation is unique to them, we all have varying priorities.

So, your financial counselor should be helping in structuring your plan according to your specific priorities and needs. Taking proper steps to build the right structure for you will safeguard your finances and extend your financial reach. It is the right choice to employ a financial partner who could advise you to do better than what you're doing now.

It is beneficial for most people to seek counsel no matter what stage of life they are in. However, there are life events that should trigger a sense of urgency, such as starting a new career, advancing in your professional life, getting married or divorced, having a child, preparing for retirement or adjusting into a newly retired routine, the death of loved one, and a host of other situations such as these.

Contingency Planning

A contingency plan can be defined as a course of action which is intended to help an organization so that it can respond effectively to an event that may occur in the future. It can also be referred to as *"Plan B."* Contingency plans are alternative actions that are taken when the results of a situation do not turn out as expected. Businesses use contingency planning to protect the business from harm, and from a disruption in operations. Procedures are put in place to manage risk and for disaster recovery. Be aware that businesses are not the only entities in need of a solid contingency plan.

Individuals who are supporting a family should also have a back-up plan for unpredictable situations they may encounter. An unforeseen situation could involve someone in your care, you, or a piece of property. What if you became disabled or dysfunctional in some way? How would this affect your life, your ability to earn an income? What about the medical expenses you could rapidly build up? The purpose of building a contingency plan is to secure you financially. Since every individual has a specific set of requirements, each person's contingency plan and budget is going to be unique to their situation.

When preparing a plan for contingencies, take a close look at your monthly expenses. See if you can *"trim the fat."* Ask yourself, can I cut back on any of my monthly bills: cable television, a cleaning service, the gardener, an extra phone line, a movie subscription, automotive expenses, etc. You also must consider your fixed monthly expenses: rent/mortgage, groceries, utility bills, business-related expenses, commute costs to work, insurance payments, etc.

You and your financial counselor must use these expenses to compile a budget that reflects how much you are saving and spending each month. Then use this as a basis to identify what expenses you could cut as your contingency budget. It is also wise to factor in extra sources of income in an emergency, which could be property or investments that you can afford to sell.

The primary reason that your financial counselor will assist you in coming up with a contingency plan and budget is so that it is ready to be implemented right away when the need arises. This plan will need to be updated periodically to account for changes in your standard budget. It is vital that you inform your counselor of any changes that you intend to make in your budget. For example, if you have eliminated your cable or satellite TV, then your financial counselor must know about it so that adjustments can be made, so you can save accordingly.

Funding Large Purchases

There are multiple times in your life when you will require large amounts of money to accomplish a goal. These milestones usually include buying a house, purchasing a car, getting married, or planning for college, just to name a few. Such events usually require you to save a substantial amount of money. To do so, you may have to determine which expenses to cut down on or eliminate altogether.

A financial counselor can assist you in creating a workable plan for saving. Unlike a contingency plan, this expense will be planned out and built into your active budget. It is best that you are as specific as possible regarding the actual amount you need and the timeframe in which you must accomplish the goal.

Estate Planning

Deciding if your situation calls for a financial planner, stockbroker, insurance agent, attorney, or accountant is a significant step in navigating your financial road map. You may already have one or more of these financial professionals guiding you. But, having a holistic financial advisor/coach/counselor could connect all these vital areas and fill in some vital gaps.

In some cases, you could be handling investments yourself, but may find it beneficial to consult with a professional to help you determine if you're saving enough for retirement. Your counselor acts as a generalist by developing a comprehensive plan that addresses all vital areas of your finances. There should be a plan addressing how your estate should be passed on in the case of your death.

The first thing to consider is whether you have a drafted Will. Do you have a document that upon death gives direction as to how you would like your assets passed on? What happens in the case that a beneficiary dies before assets are disbursed? Does that beneficiary have a Will?

Your financial and investment plan should align with your estate plan. If you have employed an attorney for your estate planning, that attorney should have direct access to your financial advisor. There should be a collaborative effort between the two to make sure that all things align.

Some estate issues can be very complex, so your financial advisor can play a vital role in your estate planning and figuring out the best possible way to pass down your life's work to your inheritors.

CHAPTER 7
YOU'RE DEAD!! NOW WHAT?

Last night I was called Home to my eternal life. As I look back over my life, I'm-anxious to see if I had lived in such a way that merits, *"A Job Well Done"* from my Lord and Savior. I want to know if he feels I was a good person, not only to my loved ones but to thine neighbors as well. I want to know if I've-made my Heavenly Father proud.

In that same vein, I want to know how my family and friends feel. Will they miss me? Will my absence be felt? What value did I bring to each and every one of them? I most certainly don't want my living to have been in vain. I could only pray that I have left behind a legacy of warm memories that will last for their lifetime. I pray that we have made enough positive memories to outweigh any negative ones we have experienced.

I pray that no one is financially suffering due to my decisions and choices. Dying is a part of any living organism's life. Every beginning has to come to an end. As established in the previous chapters, there are many ways for you to prepare for this transition. You can create as much peace in this situation as possible. It will require you to perform some tasks that you may not like, but that are necessary to undertake while you're still breathing. These steps will negate your loved ones from having to jump hurdles to carry out your desires and wishes. It will negate them from having to figure out exactly what your desires and wishes are. Facing our mortality is one of the hardest things we must do in life. It can be difficult to come face to face with the prospect of death.

However, we have to do this to protect the people we love from being ripped from their rightful inheritance. It is not wise to wait until your old age to create a Will or trust. It is in fact in everyone's best interest when you properly plan, especially when you have a family of your own. As explained previously, a trust is far easier for people to operate after the owner of the trust has passed away.

When its contents are set to be distributed among the beneficiaries as per the deceased's wishes, a trust will distribute assets more efficiently when compared with a Will. In order for you to understand exactly what you need to do in your special and specific situation, you must start planning now. It is highly recommended that you seek professional advisement to make certain that you are moving in the right direction for your particular circumstances. It is recommended that you seek the services of a Trust/Estate Planning Attorney. Be prepared to be asked some tough questions. These questions may make you uncomfortable, but they are necessary. Here are a few questions that may help you in gaining perspective on what type of information the attorney will seek to know:

- What will happen to your children if both parents passed away prior to them reaching adulthood?

A majority of people would wait until they feel their children are old enough to discuss who will inherit what and who they would want to live with if something tragic were to happen. But this is not a wise decision. If you have failed to name a guardian, then the court will do it for you. The court's decision will be based on what it deems to be the most favorable for your child.

So, always be prepared for any situation and prepare your trust and your Will so that your children won't have to go through the turmoil of not only losing a parent, or parents, but also being propelled into an undesirable living situation. Think about the fact that if you simply left a minor child as a beneficiary on a life insurance policy without leaving legally recognizable instructions as to how funds should be distributed, the funds you leave could potentially be exhausted by the appointed guardian before the child reaches legal age. The reality is, you have no control as to how your minor children are cared for if you don't plan for it beforehand.

- Are you responsible for a Special Needs Person? How have you planned and prepared for their care?
- Who will you designate as beneficiaries for all of your assets?
- Who would you want to handle all of your business affairs such as paying creditors, disbursement of funds, dissolution of

a business, etc.?

- Do you have any unborn children/heirs to consider, such as embryos?
- Who would take care of your pets?
- Who has access to your digital life? Who would you want to access and handle the dissolution of those accounts?

All your living descendants must be accounted for in your Will or your trust. This also includes children from previous marriages and descendants from other affairs. There are multiple reasons that you may want to keep those things away from your family, but it is required by law that you state and address these relationships in your Will and/or trust. It will help you in avoiding any further complications that may arise from all parties involved.

No matter how much you try to avoid the closeted descendants and affairs, they will certainly want their fair share of inheritance after you have passed away. Add to that the misery of going through endless court battles for your possessions, the shock, and the trauma that your family may have to suffer from finding out about your outside activities, you have left behind a world of devastation, hurt and disappointment. It's hard to revel in the good memories you may have created with such hurt looming in the air.

Avoiding GoFund Me!!!

Shaping the Future

People are living healthier, more active lives than ever before. They are more conscious about the food choices they make, their activities, the exercises they engage in, and how to fit they are. It leads to people having longer lifespans. There is a high possibility that many people will spend as much time in retirement as they have in their careers, which creates the possibility of outliving your retirement funds.

Living longer requires significant financial resources to ensure that you do not drain your resources before you pass away. In order to move past the stage of worrying, put a financial plan in place. It will determine your financial strengths and weaknesses. It also accounts for the expenses that you may think are small but amount to a lot when totaled. Gathering all your financial information and consolidating it into an individual plan can place you in a much better position than you would be without a financial plan.

However, your retirement should not be the only concern on your radar. You have to get past multiple stages of life first. When you know where you stand financially, you can be prepared for emergencies and opportunities, alike. In addition to that, financial planning has the ability to shape the future of your children. With all of the relatives that have passed in my family, grandparents included, no one left behind anything substantial.

One grandfather didn't believe in life insurance, thus left the family pooling funds together to pay for his funeral and burial. The other grandfather left his business in the wrong relative's hands. After his death, she proceeded to lock everyone out of his affairs. He trusted that she would divvy his assets up fairly between his heirs. She didn't relinquish anything, not even his personal items worth sentimental value. It's believed that she had him sign papers during his health decline.

None of his other children stood up to challenge her. Everyone just walked away with the confidence that karma would catch up to her, and it did. One of my grandmother's insurance policies lapsed within months of her death. So once again, loved ones were left to forgo their financial obligations in an effort to give her what we call *"a proper send-off."* In essence, if those individuals would have cared enough to properly plan, as opposed to leaving loved ones with financial challenges, they could have left a legacy that would have possibly changed the trajectory of our lives.

Equate Money with Meaning

A financial plan is a road map to your future. This plan tells you where you are presently and where you would like to get to in the future. In addition to that, you will know what steps you need to take to get to your goal. A basic financial plan will provide you with a visual that tells you whether you are on track to achieve your goals or not. If your devised plan is showing negative signs, then your road-map will need to be adjusted to align with your goals.

Your financial plan will have to be regularly monitored to ensure that you remain on track to achieve your goals. The better your plan is, the more accurately it will project how much you have to save, invest or borrow. It can also provide a timeline for your savings to accumulate and for you to obtain what you want. The accomplishment of your goals can lead you to better peace of mind and prosperity. Although wealth should not be the only criteria for happiness, it can be a contributing factor to your contentment. Furthermore, well-managed finances can protect you from various other unprecedented situations. Insurance for life, property and medical expenses allows you to have stability when things don't go as planned.

Awareness

A financial plan helps you in managing your cash flow in the most efficient manner. Since you are keeping track of your finances, you are able to manage your debt payments and identify the best way to manage it effectively. It is easy for some people to lose track of their expenses through credit card payments and online payments. This is why we sometimes spend more than we earn without even noticing. The availability of credit card lines and loans also makes us lose track of how much money we actually have, versus how much money we owe in debts.

It is always best to be aware of future obligations so that we are able to balance our cash flow accordingly. Most often our needs and financial goals change over time. Therefore, your financial plan should provide flexibility. You can alter your financial strategy so that you can meet new objectives. Reviewing your financial plan on a regular basis is crucial to keep your money in check.

The attitude of an individual also plays an important role in financial planning. Your progress is hinged upon having a positive attitude about the process. Change rarely starts off easy. It isn't until it becomes a habit does the feeling of discomfort dissipate. Your financial plan needs to be a friend that adds value to your life. Do not treat it as your enemy. It is meant to help you achieve your dreams.

Earn Respect for Generations

Most parents seek to strike the perfect balance of leaving their children enough money so that they can pursue opportunities without financial worry. However, they do not want to leave them too much for fear of spoiling them. But, if you groom your children from an early age, letting them know how important it is to have well-managed finances, more importantly how you manage your finances, they will grow up understanding the impact of being vigilant.

Now, if you have waited, you may be reluctant for your adult children to know the details of your personal finances. But you have to remind yourself that your estate plan will ultimately have a direct and likely profound impact on your children. Your children need to be made aware of the plans you have for their inheritance. This avoids surprises and ensures that any assets that will eventually be inherited are properly accounted for. Make sure that all the resources you intend to pass on are integrated into each child's wealth plan. You must develop a structured game plan for wealth transfer. In order to do so, you must be able to control the time and the method of asset distribution. If structured correctly, your plan could create a legacy for generations to come.

By simply opening up a dialogue around this issue, parents may be able to alleviate a host of pressing concerns about money, investing and finances. Irrespective of how prepared you think your children are to inherit significant wealth, you must educate them about your Will and/or your trust.

The Red Dress

Allow me to introduce you to Mike Anderson. Mike is a middle-aged over-the-road trucker who is married to Sophie, who has been a stay-at-home mom since she was pregnant with her first child, who is now 20 years old. Mike and Sophie have been blessed with two lovely and pretty accomplished daughters who are both attending college. Sarah, the oldest girl, attends The University of Houston. Mia, the youngest of the two girls, attends Baylor University. Due to an onslaught of recent fatal accidents involving truck drivers, Sophie convinced Mike to submit an application for life insurance. Mike proceeded to set an appointment with a local insurance agent. After a bit of small talk and banter, the agent began to ask Mike questions about his finances and about his health. Being the private person that he is, Mike felt somewhat uncomfortable in answering such personal questions.

The agent assured him that the details of their conversation would stay confidential, but that the answers to the questions were absolutely necessary to establish pricing and to make sure he qualified for coverage. Mike proceeded despite his uncertainty. As they exchanged dialog, Mike became more receptive to the agent.

He found the agent to be knowledgeable, and very patient. One of the questions the agent asked Mike was, *"For how long would you like to leave your income for your wife so that she won't have to change her lifestyle drastically and immediately should something happen to you?"*

Mike's answer was, *"I'm not leaving my income for her to be laying up with some other man in my house after I'm gone! No way is that happening!"*

The agent nodded and said, *"Okay, well at least leave enough money for her to go out and get a red dress."*

Mike looked puzzled and said, *"Red dress? Why would she be buying a red dress?"*

The agent said, *"Since you're not leaving her any money to live on, she's going to be forced to buy a red dress so that she can go out to find a man to come up in that house to help her pay all the bills you left her with."*

Mike couldn't say anything. All he could do was laugh. The agent proceeded to explain that if Mike left Sophie in a good position, she wouldn't need any assistance from another man. She would have the choice to remain as single and independent as she wanted to.

But leaving her with much of nothing would give her no options, especially since she hadn't worked in more than 20 years. Mike sat and pondered what the agent had said. He pictured Sophie having a tough time financially. He didn't want that for his wife of 20 years. He wanted her to have peace in his absence, not financial turmoil. He picked up the ink pen to sign the application that would change the trajectory of his family's future completely.

To the Readers

Let's say you had a tree in your backyard which was a 100 years old with $100 bills hanging from its branches. Surely, this majestic beauty is now considered a monument for the property. You would not want this tree harmed in any way since it holds so much value, you will surely need to protect it. But how do you protect it? You could barb wire it and place armed guards around it.

However, what if you were too late to put that barbed wire up and now the tree has been harmed or worse, it has been destroyed and robbed of its riches? There is nothing you can do now that the moment to protect it has passed. All you can do is blame the person who harmed it or even sue them to recover the damages they caused. But none of that will make up for the mistake you made of neglecting to protect the tree.

Maybe you had not planned for the tree to live as long as it did, or you didn't think it mattered enough. Now imagine if the tree were a person who had no life insurance. The barbed wire would be the protection that life insurance provides you and your family while you are living, as well as after you have passed away.

YOU ARE THE MONEY TREE!

So dear readers, it is always best to get yourself insured so that you live a comfortable life knowing that your family won't suffer immensely even after they lose your shadow. In addition to that, a financial plan will provide you a close analysis of your finances and allow you to enjoy life while saving cautiously. Saving money does not mean that you have to put a damper on the fun.

Remember this quote from Benjamin Franklin,

"If you fail to plan, you are planning to fail."

Always plan ahead and plan to win!

Good luck!